Animal Life after Death
& Animal Reincarnation

Answers for your Heart's Questions!
Plus, learn "how to" see, feel, communicate
& connect with your deceased pet.

BRENT ATWATER

Copyright information © 2008-2015 by B. Brent Atwater
Published and Distributed in the United States by:
Brent Atwater's Just Plain Love® Books
www.BrentAtwater.com

Editorial: Brent Atwater
Interior Design: Brent Atwater

Cover Design: Brent Atwater
Illustrations: Brent Atwater

All rights reserved. No part of this book may be reproduced by any mechanical, photographic or electronic process or in the form of a phonographic reading: nor may it be stored in a retrieval system transmitted, or otherwise be copied for public or private use- other than for "fair use" as brief quotations embodied in articles and reviews without prior written permission of the publisher and author.

The contents presented herein are derived from the author's intuition and experiences. The intent of the author is only to offer information of a general nature to help facilitate your journey to health and well-being. In the event you choose to use any of the information in this book for yourself, which is your constitutional right, there are no guarantees and the author and the publisher assume no responsibility for your actions.

Library of Congress Cataloging-in-Publication Data

Paperback ISBN:9781503067929

Hardcover ISBN:
EBook ISBN:
Kindle: ASIN:
Audio:
R1

Translated into multiple languages.

Printing 1: 2015 USA
Canada
UK, AU, EU, SA check with distributor
Publisher's Price Higher in Other Countries

Visit Brent Atwater's Web site
www.BrentAtwater.com

This *Just Plain Love*® Book
is given
To: _____

Message: _____
Date: _____

with
LOTS of LOVE, HUGS and KISSES!!!

From: _____

& "**Friend**"

Acknowledgements

I want to thank you the reader
for taking the time to explore my
Just Plain Love® Books
and for allowing me to share what I have learned
and am learning about pet loss, death, pet life after
death, pet reincarnation and animal communication
through other individuals and
my personal experiences.

Special thanks to Michael Wellford
and my precious fur, finned and feathered
companions for their contributions and enduring
patience with me and my spiritual path.

It is my intent
that this information will facilitate
inspiration, greater perspectives and
expanded awareness in your life.

I thank those who have supported and encouraged
my journey
and the authors, speakers and teachers
who contributed to shaping my consciousness.

My gratitude also goes to:
Each individual who has shared their story with me
so our readers can derive hope and be inspired by
"all that is."

A special thank you to
all the pets, animals and their guardians
whose never ending love bond represents
why I write my pet life after death and
pet reincarnation books.

Dedication

This book is written to honor my entire inspiring and
beloved canine, feline, equine and other animal
teachers, guardians and companions
(including "Fishy") with whom I shared
my experiences, learning and life.
From my heart and soul to yours, thank you!

My special love goes to each and every one of you
for filling my life and heart with joy.

To Thomas Michael Ramseur Wellford,
whose life, love and passing
made my understanding possible.
I shall always hold you
and hear you in my heart,
my soul and my dreams.

To those very special people and fur babies
who are my joy,
and with whom I share
hope, laughter and LIFE!!!

Animal Life after Death & Animal Reincarnation
Everything You Always Wanted to Know!

TABLE OF CONTENTS

Personalized Message & Gift Page	vii
Acknowledgments	ix
Dedication	xi
Table of Contents	13
I want to say	15
The Dog with a "B" on His Bottom!	17
History of Reincarnation	21
Reincarnation is a Simple Concept	27
Pet Loss & Physical Death is the Beginning	29
The Transition Process	30
Signs the Transition Process Has Begun	31
Affirmation to Assist in Transition	32
Memory Moments	35
The Importance of Believing in Reincarnation	36
How to Ask Your Pet if It's Going to Come back	37
Initial Grief	38
Pet Loss Grief Groups: Positive or Negative	41
Can I Talk My Pet Into Coming Back?	46
How to Assist a Pet in Reincarnating	46
How Many Times Can An Animal Reincarnate?	48
What is My Animal's Purpose?	53
"God" Animals	57
3 Types of Reincarnation	65
How Long Does Reincarnation Take?	71
Can I Renegotiate Our Agreement?	73
What is an "Over Soul" Agreement?	79
Can a Pet Return as a Human?	81

Brent Atwater's
Just Plain Love® Books presents

Pet Life after Death & "I'm Home!"	85
Ways to Communicate with a Deceased Pet	85
What Can Affect Communication with My Pet?	85
The Difference in AC and AIH Readings	87
Is Contacting My Pet's Energy Selfish?	88
How to Bring Your Pet's Energy to Earth	91
How to Touch Your Deceased Pet's Energy	97
How to Locate a Lost Pet	101
How to See a Pet's Aura and Spirit	103
What Can Prohibit My Pet from Visiting Me?	106
Memorials, Gravesites and Altars	109
Return from Rainbow Bridge Poems	111
Signs from a Deceased Pet	121
Do These Signs Mean My Pet is coming Back?	126
Stages of Bereavement	129
Grieving	129
Anger	130
Guilt	132
Reconnection: How Do I Find My Pet?	133
Recognition: Could I Miss My Pet?	135
Confirmation: How Will I Know It's MY Pet?	139
Reuniting: "I'm Home!"	145
Your Reincarnated Pet	147
Questions from the Audience	151
Pet Loss Support & Reincarnation Resources	171
Message to Book Clubs & Associations	174
About the Author	175
The Just Plain Love® Story	178
Other Just Plain Love® Titles	181

I want to say

If you are reading this introduction you're probably an animal lover or someone you know needs a GREAT BIG HUG!

If you just plain love® animals or have experienced the loss of a beloved furry, feathered or finned soul mate, have an interest in animal communication, pet past lives, animal soul contracts, afterlife, animal spirits and reincarnation, or care about someone who is grieving over the loss of their pet companion, this is the world's #1 resource to answer **your** questions!

Animal Life after Death answers almost everything you can think of about pet loss, transition, pet life after death and the animal reincarnation process. It teaches you how to ask your pet if they are going to come back, ways to get in touch with your pet on the other side and also recognize them when they return to earth. Plus there are techniques that teach you "how to" sense, see, touch and communicate with your deceased pet.

True Animal Reincarnation stories can be found in my *"I'm Home!" a Never Ending Love Story* books for Dogs, Cats and Horses. These stories illustrate the various signs and reincarnation events which led to reuniting each pet parent with their beloved companions.

Ms. Atwater offers her dog Friend's past lives and multiple reincarnations in her lifetime as the foundation of all "I know from my heart and soul's experiences during each of my beloved pets' sickness, degenerating health, disease, chronic illness and even sudden or inevitable death to crossing over the Rainbow Bridge and coming back.

I want to thank all God's wonderful and cherished creatures who have taught me what I share with you in this book that I write to honor all their lives.

I have written in a conversational manner, to enhance the emotional connections. I chose not to be limited by strict traditional editing parameters. Since writing is an art, I'm allowed that creative expression.

Brent Atwater's
Just Plain Love® Books presents

This book derives its information from my research and a multitude of international interspecies before and after life stories gathered over decades. The pet reincarnation stories are the embodiment of lessons pet parents learned and how their heart's awareness evolved to a higher consciousness through experiencing each death and rebirth.

"Reliving each story inside my heart while checking the formatting, spelling and editing of this book was difficult. I hope my continuing research will give peace to your heart and support what you are going though, plus provide and extend what you are seeking to learn.

It is my intent that this book comforts you, reassures your soul's knowing and helps ignite hope, in addition to providing healing insight that expands your awareness to all things possible and real!

I expect these true stories will give you tingles and goose bumps (a friend calls them God bumps) of confirmation and that you can relate to the thoughts, feeling and experiences of each owner and perhaps think

Hummmmmm,

that relates to what's going on in my life!

If someone has told you "it's just a pet, get over it," I hope each of you will experience profound healing from the expanded awareness you have embraced when your beloved animal companions reincarnate to be with you again."

After Death Signs

from

Pet Afterlife & Animals in Heaven

How to Ask for Signs & Visits
and What They Mean

BRENT ATWATER
Animal Medium

the **Dog with MY "B" on His Bottom!**

My investigation into death and afterlife began almost 20 years ago when I lost my fiancé in an unexpected auto accident. I desperately wanted to find him.

Brent Atwater's
Just Plain Love® Books presents

I started researching ways that his energy could return to me.

While studying afterlife, life after death and the reincarnation process, I became more and more aware that my dogs demonstrated similar if not downright exact character traits of each other.

"Friend" my border collie was born with a white "B" on his bottom that exactly matches my signature. I took that as my sign and mission to write about what my heart had come to know to be true-
Pet life after death and Pet Reincarnation is real!

While furthering my investigations and documenting the evidence I was collecting, I gathered true stories from around the world. Each one taught me more about afterlife, reincarnation and the animal kingdom. I read about live pets that had reincarnated multiple times within each owner's life, like Friend had done in mine. Others validated and illustrated before and after death examples of each of the signs and events within the reincarnation process.

I wrote my *"I'm Home!"* companion books for readers to be able to touch each animal whose story is in that book. I want the reader to be able to talk to each pet's guardian to hear "their story," so no one could say I "made this stuff up!"

This *Animal Life after Death* book represents insights derived from evidence found time and time again from all the shared stories and questions asked in TV and radio interviews, my groups, workshops, lectures, presentations and book signings that I have done and will do.

Whenever I think that I have covered E-V-E-R-Y question, another one comes along. I revise this book almost every year to reflect my latest and most current knowledge. Based upon requests by readers, I also add new animal communication and connection techniques to each revision.

It is my intent for this book **to empower you** to communicate with and understand your pet's energy before, during and after life and to be able to connect with them throughout their transition and reincarnation process.

That's also why I founded the process of how to see inside of an animal's body and to track your pet's life force energy from their current physical form, through transition into life after death and their reincarnation evolution.

I was a non-believer in all this "other side stuff" until Mike's death showed me "all that is." Because I trusted him in life, I trusted him in death to teach me what I now share with you.

I want to educate readers that pet life after death and animal reincarnation is real!

The History of Reincarnation

Reincarnation is believed to occur when the spirit or soul, after biological death, comes back to earth in a new body to experience more learning.

The belief in Reincarnation dates back as far as the ancient Egyptians. Others that embrace reincarnation are the Buddhist, Hindu, Jainism, Indian and Taoism religions including historic figures such as Plato and Socrates. Simply put, when you believe in reincarnation that means you believe that a soul's life force energy is immortal i.e. ongoing and infinite.

Animal reincarnation is sometimes called transmigration; a process that the Hindu religion, Yogic view and others endorse. The transmigration process is the belief that the spirit/ soul of the deceased body passes into successive bodily forms. According to the Yogic view an animal must transmute many times to evolve into a human form.

The most popular reincarnation definition believes when one's physical body dies their life force energy known as the "spirit" or "soul" is everlasting. Therefore that soul can choose to be reborn into another body.

It's also a common belief that the new body the old soul chooses to inhabit is based on its past life Karma and its karmic purpose or spiritual arrangement with you. Therefore to me, it is a reasonable expectation that many people would believe their pets will reincarnate.

Although not all people believe in reincarnation; it's interesting that most people agree that you will be with all your pets that have gone to the Rainbow Bridge when your body dies and your spirit crosses to the other side.

In 2007 a respected British leading independent research company YouGov conducted a study and found that dogs proved to be the type of animal most likely to be considered reincarnated by pet owners: 51% said they had or have dogs that they believe reincarnated while 44% said their cat returned.

Some individuals, who have not experienced a reincarnated pet, feel that pets do not return because they have no need to or that the animals don't have lessons to learn.

Others who have not experienced a reincarnated angel animal suggest that a deceased loved one who passed may have sent you a special furry, finned or feathered baby to be with you. In my investigations and experience, animals reincarnate for diverse reasons.

A soul connected forever pet is usually a spiritual teacher, guide or guardian spirit that travels with you in pet form throughout your earthly journey.

The reincarnation information herein was researched and gathered from friends, clients, myriad stories and testimonials in addition to my personal experiences. We all believe that in my dog Friend's and each of our individual's pet's life and in whatever form they choose, animals DO reincarnate!

Use any information that resonates with you and remember-

There can always be exceptions!

© Return from Rainbow Bridge Video

When you've lost your beloved pet, service animal, companion, assistance dog, therapy pet, soul pet partner and forever finned, feathered or fur baby, - "love of your life," your "heart and soul and everything good in the world" "child," **don't lose hope!** Listen to your heart's urgings, watch your dreams and follow your soul's knowing. Since your pet is a part of the tapestry of your life and every fiber of your being, pay attention to your intuition and inner guidance.

If you feel that you want to or must hold onto your pet's beds, belongings and toys, even saving their fur in a jar, **there is a reason**. If you whispered while they were on their deathbed "come back to me" **there is a reason!** If your heart says where is my pet, where is my pet, I have to find him! Some part of your soul's inner being knows that they **will** be back.

Brent Atwater's
Just Plain Love® Books presents

Each and every animal's Soul is a spirit composed of eternal life force energy that lives forever in our vast Universe. Whether or not it's your soul pet, forever fur baby, animal spirit guide or spiritual teacher in an animal form, God/ the Universe honors your pet's choice to reincarnate in whatever way to be with you in various physical bodies throughout your life time.

Why does a pet come back / reincarnate?

Coming back to share life with you again is NOT about your animal's soul's purpose or singular lessons, or that you want him well in this lifetime, or because you love each other so much. Your pet's coming back to you in a new body or other reincarnation forms is about **what you have to learn together**.

He/she will continue to reincarnate, "walk in," or "soul braid" until <u>your combined learning</u> opportunities and spiritual agreements are fulfilled. Animal reincarnation is about the human animal soul contract that you made BEFORE your return to Earth for this and other lifetimes. That reincarnation contract **is just between the two of you and no one else.**

KNOW your pet's Soul energy is never gone forever. He's just changed from the physical form into living energy without a body.

Give your animal's life force energy time to recover, recalibrate, regenerate and restore in order to choose or relocate in a new body if they have agreed to return. You can always communicate with them throughout the entire process.

A reincarnation contract is not complicated.
All forms of reincarnation accomplish the fact that your pet is back to share with you in the eternal cycle of life.

The "come back" process of reentry and timing may create some twists and turns, but it's a simple soul to soul contract. **It's an agreement to return only to you.**

Your soul will know when it's time to look for your pet again.

**Follow your heart,
you can't miss them!**

Together you begin AGAIN,

Brent Atwater's
Just Plain Love® Books presents

Here's an Affirmation to open the **possibility** for pet reincarnation:

"I celebrate your Love and set my Grief free, so You can choose to come back to me."

"I celebrate your Love and set my Grief free, so You can choose to come back to me!"

© Animal Reincarnation Animal Life After Death by Brent Atwater

*** Even though you wish it so with all your heart, **NO affirmation** will insure that your pet will come back or create a reincarnation contract.

Do animals ALWAYS come back?
Sometimes one lifetime is all you both chose to experience together.

How many pets come back or reincarnate?
For almost 20 years my Guides say only 30 to 40 percent of pets reincarnate. They ONLY come back to learn and share more Soul evolving lessons with you. **If you don't have a lesson to learn together then they do not come back!**

* Reincarnation Is A Simple Concept! *

If you boil WATER, what does it make? STEAM
If you freeze STEAM, what does it become?
ICE CRYSTALS! If you melt ICE CRYSTALS,
what does it become?   WATER!
And so the **never ending energy cycle** goes on!

Life force/ Soul energy NEVER changes!
It just **changes into different physical FORMS.**

It's physics! Electromagnetic energy never dies.
Think about the water- ice- steam concept!
The energy base of water never goes away;
it just changes into different physical forms.

Did you know that the human body is made up of
about 75% water and a cat's body about 60%?
According to the ASPCA water makes up to 80 % of
your dog's body weight.

Brent Atwater's
Just Plain Love® Books presents

You might want to think of a pet that has left his original body as being in "steam" form at the Rainbow Bridge until he chooses another physical form for his return trip.

R I P means Reincarnation is possible!

Pet Loss - Physical Death is just the Beginning of changing energy forms and coming back to you!

Each biological body provides an opportunity to depart, whether it ages, is physically broken or ill, just wears out or opts out early during birth or the newborn process.
Death begins the trading physical forms process. A soul's energy NEVER dies, it just changes forms!
Due to shorter life spans, upgrading to a healthier body is a necessity for our beloved animals, birds, fish or reptiles so they can continue sharing your life's journey.

Like Humans, animals have multiple exit points that they can choose to use to leave. That's why "when its time," you and your pet inherently understand what's going on. It's a script you **both agreed to** for this exit point and learning opportunity. No matter how gentle or horrific your pet's transition is, remember, **you and your pet chose this specific scenario to enhance each soul's growth.**

Brent Atwater's
Just Plain Love® Books presents

If you are reading this book prior to the impending passage of the "love of your life," KNOW that death and transition is the **FIRST** step in reuniting with you.

Death is NOT forever, it's just FOR A WHILE!

Those factual words will help you during transition and the waiting process. It will save a lot of tears to you wait in anticipation and not grief.

The Transition Process

During the transition process, your pet's physical body will be in conflict with its soul's love for you. He will want to stay on Earth to emotionally support you although everyone understands that's not possible.

Sometimes when a pet is preparing to pass and you subliminally want them to "hang on" for your sake:

>The pet will walk away or distance themselves from you,
>Not look at you in your eyes,
>Avoid their normal personal contact habits,
>Stay or hide in another room trying to avoid the conflicting energy.

Another sign of impending transition is when you see an older or sickly pet sitting at a window or door just staring out as if they are memorizing their last earthly view.

They are!

Do not have any guilt about the death process. Remember, whatever occurred was "scripted" and agreed upon between your souls before it happened. Your pet knew and knows he was/ is loved and that you were/are doing the best you could/can do. If the death was "an accident" that scenario was planned too. KNOW that everything is **EXACTLY as it should have been for the lessons and learning opportunities** you each contracted to experience.

Signs that Physical Transition is Imminent

Usually 24 – 48 hours prior to leaving its body your pet's Soul will start to withdraw its life force energy. If you can see energy, their aura will gradually diminish. During that time or beforehand

Brent Atwater's
Just Plain Love® Books presents

you can ask your pet if it is going to reincarnate.
If you see auras (a field of subtle, luminous radiation surrounding a person, pet or object like a halo), you will be able to notice your animal's electromagnetic life force energy (aura) becoming more centrally organized near the heart area. During that time an animal's physical body becomes colder as their energy is being incrementally withdrawn in preparation for departure. This progressive physical process starts as cold paws and ears, pale gums, then lackluster or nonresponsive eyes, etc.

If you can track and see life force energy (dead pet spirits) as I do, you will see an animal draw his aura energy inside of his body.   Then your pet's aura will begin to have lots of black holes in it. When the pet's energy becomes totally black, at that time, you know their life force energy has completed transition and detached from its body. You will then watch whirling purple energy rotating in an upward counter clock wise direction as their life force essence crosses the death line, a solid black area, before reappearing on the life after death side as a bright white sparkler light in "all there is."

Affirmation to assist a pet's transition
The affirmation below will assist your cherished companion in transitioning easier and without horrific physical complications.
1. Hold its front paws with your hands or place the hand that you write with (that's your energy sending hand) on the pet's body near its heart. If this is difficult to do it's not imperative.
2. Look into your pet's eyes if possible but not necessary. **Ask within your heart or voice out loud:** (Say one time or as often as you wish.)

Your intent will assist in making your pet's transition as gentle as possible. **Do not change the wording or it will change the type of energy sent**.

"Fill in blank with Pet's name, I love you.
I honor, respect and support your choices.
From the love in my heart, I send you my life force energy to use as you so choose."

It is imperative that you use the words **"as you so choose"** so your pet can use that additional energy boost to either cross over or to get better--- Then it's THEIR choice!

An animal like a human has several predetermined exit point choices within their lifetime. Your pet can choose to survive and stay at this exit point or cross. That concept goes hand in hand with the phase about a cat's nine lives.

Remember, no matter what **you** desire, there is a point beyond which any physical body can NOT regenerate or recover.

Memory Moments!

If your pet has decided to leave or at some point in time before they cross to Rainbow Bridge, your pet will create a tender *Memory Moment*. It's their way of acknowledging your love as they complete this incarnation. You might not recognize it at first, but in hindsight it will be a vivid beloved *Memory Moment!*

A *Memory Moment* is an action or behavior that is out of character for the way your pet normally behaves or has been acting.
Example: one pet sat and stared deeply into it owner's eyes for several days before he passed. Another pet would lie on the other side of the terrace; trying to distance their energy from their pet parents. Our Pet Loss Radio Show on Pet Life Radio "*Alive Again*" has a great podcast on this.

A *Memory Moment* is also your pet's way of letting you know that everything is Ok- no matter what happens, and that he KNOWS he will be fine!

Brent Atwater's
Just Plain Love® Books presents

A client's cat was extremely ill for months and stayed alone in her bed in a dark corner. Several days after the client started saying the affirmation above, her cat got up, came over to sit in her lap and purred for the first time since her illness began. Later that night she calmly went to sleep (unassisted) in the safe haven of her owner's love while her guardian was stating this affirmation.

When you give your living pet your life force energy during the transition process, does that energy continue to work when they have crossed?
No. Since they have electromagnetically detached from their old physical body you will need to reestablish another connection with them in afterlife.

The energy and intent that you sending when they are on the other side are based upon a different frequency range. In order to access future energy to help them reincarnate you will use different prayers and intent.

Is it important to believe in reincarnation?
Yes. Your open mind facilitates the return of your pet more readily. Disbelief creates an energetic barrier, like a closed mind stops learning opportunities.

If you do not completely believe in reincarnation yet might entertain the concept and hold the thought that "at least I'll give it a try, why not?" This way, your pet can come back more easily if it has chosen to do so.

Until you open your mind to the possibility of their return, your pet will <u>not</u> reincarnate.
Why? They are honoring your free will thought process of disbelief in reincarnation.

If you choose not to believe that pets can come back and you and your pet have scheduled a return in this lifetime, the Universe will provide many situations to assist you with an "opportunity" to change your mind to complete your spiritual agreement with your animal. If your Soul doesn't evolve to embracing the possibility of reincarnation, you will need to complete that contract in another life.

How to ask your pet if it's going to come back

When you want to ask your **living** pet if it's going to reincarnate, hold its front paws with your hands or

Brent Atwater's
Just Plain Love® Books presents

place your hand on the pet's body near its heart, look into its eyes if possible and ask within your heart or out loud:

I ask and it is my intent to know if _____ and I will be together again in this lifetime.
Will _____ return to live with me again in this lifetime?
Your heart will hear the answer.

If you do not receive an answer or an answer that you feel is clear and factual, it could be due to the emotional upheaval that everyone is experiencing. Use the prayers set forth in a later section, to receive a response after your pet is on the other side.

Initial Grief

If you are reading this book immediately after the passing of your pet, don't get angry or frustrated that you can't hear what you want to know or have trouble with the various techniques connecting with your pet.

Although grief is part of the emotional process, extreme or unnaturally prolonged grief will interfere with your ability to connect with your pet.
Have **no expectations** for the initial outcome.

Intense emotions can create an energetic filter that hampers a good sending and receiving energy signal for connection and information.

Once your emotions are less intense, revisit all of these techniques and you **will be able** to do them with a little practice. **It takes about 2 weeks to connect with the other side "on demand."**

Although physical death is very heart wrenching and may seem permanent, you *must remember* They need to shed that old body for a newer better version!

Since your beloved companion is so connected to you, **chronic crying depletes your pet's regenerative energy and hampers their ability to transition back to** you in the best way possible!

Give your "baby" permission to do **as they so choose** when trying to connect with them.
    Honor their journey's timeframe from death to relife so they can be a part of yours quicker! Although this is so hard to do in critical times,
it's all about mutual love and respect.
    Focusing your attention and emotions on the DEATH of your pet accompanied by ongoing extreme grief will slow down and repel your pet's re-entry process!
    Celebrate the love you share! Focus on each precious memory and relive all the wonderful things you shared. **Savor the fact that their Love is Never Ending, their energy is Alive and well!** Reminder your pet is just in "sparkler" or Spirit form.

Pet Loss Grief Support Groups

Support groups for Rainbow Bridge residents come in all sizes and flavors; in person, in healthcare facilities, in church, in homeless pet shelters, recovery groups, animal rescue groups, in other organizations, chat rooms and online. They are promoted to provide positive emotional and spiritual support.

Ask yourself a tough question: Does your pet loss group meet the criteria for a positive or negative experience?

A positive and proactive support group is one that encourages learning, promotes going forward and helps facilitate expanded awareness and your

Brent Atwater's
Just Plain Love® Books presents

empowerment. They are a blessing in your life!

The positive group leader is not intimidated by unanswerable questions, but inspired to become more educated and find more resources and options. This moderator encourages you to ask questions that require further investigation in order to challenge each group member to think beyond the present pet loss "was" circumstances and into a larger mindset of "is it possible my pet could reincarnate?"

A positive animal bereavement group discourages group members from maintaining a "my pet is gone forever" victim mentality. It is aware of the psychological reasons you might be using your negative reaction for "sympathy attention." They understand this is a confusing and complicated time in your life. Animal Hope Counselors™ offer uplifting approaches to addressing your new life without your cherished pet.

A positive moderator's job is to facilitate your moving through this time of emotional pain and loneliness and not to enable self-pity and ongoing anguish.

From the introductory "pet loss story" to a weekly "how are you doing," crying and tales of woe, the negative pet loss support group meets only to celebrate the identity you create from the devastating death of your pet. This is the highest level of support disguise, a "victim" group, bonding and commiserating in perpetual negative energy experiences.

No matter how much you think this group is helping you cope, they are NOT.
They exist to talk about and share negative happenings thereby creating a "stuck in grief" atmosphere. It's bonding by **ongoing** "downers."

Participating in a group that does nothing but

recount what "was" and continual unhappiness subconsciously depresses and negatively impacts each participant's spirit. Your pet's death details and suffering do **not** need to be addressed over and over, again and again!

Continuous mourning with no positive solutions offered other than "poor you, I understand because my......." is a common scenario in Online groups.

I have been removed from several pet loss groups because I posted "Have you ever considered the 6000 year old concept of pet reincarnation that's been embraced by all the world's oldest and largest religions?"

Multiple individuals have told me they are afraid to ask questions about pet afterlife and reincarnation in their pet loss group because the members are repeating the same conversations (only with more Rainbow Bridge photos) for months and years!!!

Research substantiates that recounting your horror story and reading the countless painful venting of others does not facilitate positive mental health.

Acceptance is one thing, denial another. Being "the victim" of your pet's death drains your personal energy and life vitality. It may elicit help for a while, but the key here is "for a while." You are in charge of your own grief recovery!

When you free your mind of grief limitations, only then can your pet change its energy's direction and choose to come back to you.

As long as you are recounting what "was," you are living in the past. I know folks who are still telling the same story about "Fluffy's" death with every tiny detail embellished to the fullest just to keep the conversation vibrant with the drama of what "was."

To this type of person, actually moving forward after their bereavement "oh no," that pet guardian would need to have a life and do something other

Brent Atwater's
Just Plain Love® Books presents

than focus on themselves and their loss.

This type of individual moves from person to person, support group to support group until that cluster of listeners isn't asking enough questions, or providing enough "poor you" comments.

I know a woman who after years of pet loss bereavement counseling and therapy and ten years in every pet loss grief support group, animal condolence community and pet loss sympathy online forum, message board and chat room she could find, started her own pet support group because no one wanted to hear her repetitive stories.

Here's another hard question. Do you have any of the tendencies mentioned above? Do you like the attention your sorrow facilitates? If yes is your answer, then you need to determine "why" you require this form of negative attention. This inner void will erode your soul and eventually your health.

Do not use the fact that you lost your pet as an identification marker or to give your online life or chat room character significance.

By creating your identity as the suffering victim of your pet's death, YOU are the only one who will lose friends and the respect and patience of those who encourage and support your healing.

Analyze your support group's dynamics to determine if you are growing or JUST rehashing to the max. Unless YOU choose to grow forward, you will perpetually remain in the same grief condition.

Have you ever considered asking: "Have you ever contemplated that your pet does NOT have to live forever as an Angel Animal, or resident of the Rainbow Bridge in animal spirit or afterlife?

Maybe, your questions and open-minded awareness is the beginning of "**good grief**!"

I understand a traumatizing death. My fiancé was killed in a sudden auto crash. I never had the chance to say or do anything.

You CAN tell your pet loss story as a "learning opportunity" to help educate and heal others rather than as a commiseration Band-Aid. Although grieving takes time, uplifting attitudes are essential.

It's better to celebrate your fur baby's life and remember all the good times. **By celebrating your pet's positive contribution to your life, you never have to bury the memories they made with you.** You can take them out of your heart's memory box at any time, like a special gift and savor all the wonderful thoughts and feelings.

Brent Atwater's
Just Plain Love® Books presents

Can I talk my pet into coming back?
I know a woman that wanted her pet to reincarnate immediately after death. The pet complied with her wishes. He arrived in poor health and was sickly his entire life.

It's selfish to rush timing. The results from rushing the reincarnation process "perfect timing" can be less than desirable.

Be patient in order for your pet to make the most appropriate and healthiest reentry.

To honor your pet, know it's **their** soul's choice. The spiritual agreement made between you was contracted before you entered this life. To request a revision of your previous agreement could promote unhealthy Karma.

"the Dog with a "B" on His Bottom" about my dog Friend was written to prove that your prayers will be answered in perfect timing! "B"elieve and "B" inspired to hold onto your hope.

Can anything help a pet to return to you "sooner rather than later?"
Your contract of "when and how to meet" **was made prior to coming to Earth.** After the appropriate learning has been accomplished and at the exact time you each agreed, your reincarnation contract will be fulfilled. Sometimes the only "sooner or later" variable is about the lessons learned and growing your soul opportunities, or you renegotiating a later date due to free will choices.

How to Assist Your Pet in the Reincarnation Process

This prayer is similar to supporting your pet in making their transition more smoothly.
However, in order to create another outcome, your intent is different.

I ask and it is my intent to send _____ (the deceased pet's name) from the love in my heart, my life force energy to use as you so choose. So be it, it is done. Thank you.

The love in your heart transcends all realms. IF you and your pet have made another agreement for this incarnation, using this prayer will provide the extra energy boost to help them realign for reentry. It will also assist their transition back to earth more easily.

The key is to state these exact words:
"**to use as you so choose."** Then your pet will determine the perfect timing for their healthy return ONLY IF they are scheduled to do so.

NO amount of wanting, hope or wishful thinking, affirmations or prayers will bring your pet back, UNLESS you already have a contract in place.

A Soul's Energy NEVER changes!
It just changes into different physical FORMS.

Prayer to ask for Reincarnation Confirmation Signs

I ask and it is my intent to know if _____ is going to return to be with me in this lifetime.

Please give me 3 signs within the next three days that I can easily understand that will allow me to know in my heart if my beloved pet is coming back to me in this lifetime. Thank you.

How many times can an animal reincarnate?
Each pet has its individual soul's path as you do. Sometimes a pet has agreed to be with you **only** once in your entire life. That single incarnation has a purpose and is their "path" and contract with you.

Brent Atwater's
Just Plain Love® Books presents

You will know within your heart if your pet is returning. It's an undeniably strong and compelling feeling!

You will also sense if he isn't reincarnating. Your soul bond and intuition creates this "knowing."

Why do some pets come back and others don't? If a pet comes to earth to learn personal lessons, it usually inhabits only one incarnation.

Sometimes your pet will reincarnate many times WITH you and learn their lessons **while** sharing their experiences with you.

Friend with the "B" on his bottom got stolen from my locked car, escaped during rush hour traffic and was run over. He suffered multiple broken ribs, bleeding lungs, shifted intestines and a horrific detailed black tire tread mark implanted in his beautiful white ruff. Medically, he should not be alive today. It was his lesson to think and "B" more discerning with his hugs to strangers while spreading the word about reincarnation.

Who chooses how many times an animal reincarnates?
Before you come to earth, both of you determine how many incarnations you will share together each lifetime. It's all about the soul lessons you each want to learn on the "earth school."

The more learning and teaching you have to experience **together** (key word), the more often your pet will reincarnate to evolve with you.

If you feel that your pet is part of the "fiber of your being", or you have a "special heart connection" unlike other pets you've had, most likely you've shared many lifetimes and multiple reincarnations!

What if my pet doesn't want to come back?
Then you don't have a reincarnation contract.
 The only ways your agreement can be changed is:
Your pet can delay their entry to a more appropriate time if you are having difficult issues.
You can also ASK you pet to delay their reincarnation. Either way, if you have a contract, it must be fulfilled.

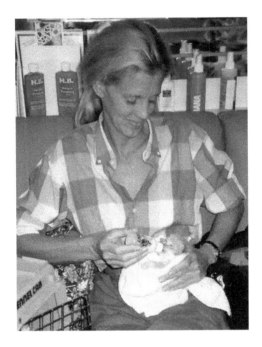

Why do young animals leave?

Sometimes a baby, adolescent or young animal that has an unexplained death or sudden onset medical problems or severe health issues will choose an early exit point. These pets get rid of their "sick" body early in life to exchange it for a healthier one. Or they might be "coming in" for a quick check on you. Later they will reincarnate in a more durable form to share a longer lifetime.

"Finding Gunner" in *"I'm Home!" a Cat's Never Ending Love Story* will warm your heart about a kitten who kept trying to get back to her guardian!

What is my Animal's Purpose?

An animal's purpose or soul contract can be a separate issue from reincarnation.

If an an animal is on its own learning journey and you interface with them, the purpose is the general evolvement of all those involved.

If you have contracted to reincarnate together, it may be to learn with you, live with you during a specific phase of your life, teach you lessons, experience a lesson themselves, save your life, teach you emotions or how to love, provide an opportunity for you to learn animal communication, volunteer at pet healthcare facilities, script a law to benefit others, start a rescue group, raise funds for pet causes, start one or a multitude of other purposes. *Never discount* any new feelings of what you "might want to do" after their lifetime because that inspiration could be the purpose!

Brent Atwater's
Just Plain Love® Books presents

Do animals come to me because our paths were meant to cross?
I'm a believer in "there are no coincidences." Every event in our lives is a learning opportunity no matter what our human side calls it. Some of my greatest educational and heartfelt experiences I learned from observing or interacting with animals in life. I wasn't "soul connected" to them, I was a student.

Evaluate the relationships you've experienced with animals. Ask yourself what you learned- good, bad or ugly and determine how it benefitted you or others. That will provide the answer about their purpose in your life.

A companion animal's purpose is to stay with their guardian during major stress events, disability, illness or end of life.
One touching story was about a stray kitten that just "showed up!" It came to sit in her owner's lap while she was wheelchair bound during the end stage diseases of her life. When the owner passed, within 3 days, that perfectly healthy cat died in her sleep to join her owner.

Animal empaths reincarnate to mirror a medical condition or to alleviate issues for its owner.
Often times an animal empath's medical plight will help the guardian learn more about treating their own disorder. Animal Empaths also assist in diffusing any unhealthy energy in their parent's environment or body.

Cats are more energy sensitive than dogs. Many take on and absorb their owner's stress or negativity which can create disease or be fatal for the feline.

Can animals have other purposes within a reincarnation?

Yes! Another type of animal soul contract or spiritual purpose with a human is called "Karmic." A karmic contract affects destiny within a single incarnation.

A Karmic contract in a particular lifetime can still be a segment of a larger soul group purpose. Ex: A Seeing Eye guide dog that leads survivors out of a building during 911. A therapy cat that inspires an assisted living home's Alzheimer's patients to speak for the first time in many years. Even an old horse can still change lives by participating in Riding for the Disabled or Handicapped Riding Programs. At 31, my Midnight was still being brushed and fed carrots by the children he was helping with his gentle ways. These experiences affect both the human's destiny AND the animal's Karma.

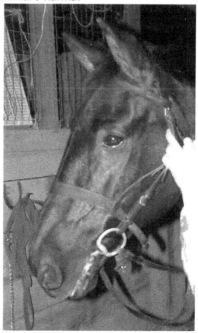

© Diane Lewis Photography

"God" Animals are a very special variety of old souls that have a significant purpose within a specific incarnation. They are "all knowing" animals that usually come for a major lesson, cause or event. They shepherd souls thru life's emotional, traumatic and life altering experiences.

The term "God Animal" and its definition were given to me by my Guides during many animal communication sessions. The Guides explained that God Animals are like "Special Forces from the Universe" that come to teach, influence and shape people's lives and situations for the highest and greatest good.

The Energy Field of a God Animal is bigger than any normal pet's aura. You can feel their presence across a room. Others will just come up and say, "There's something special" about that dog, cat or horse or… When you're in the presence of or even see a picture or video of this old soul, you can sense it!

God Animals are Leaders and Master Teachers!
God Animals can be an emotional and educational catalyst for the rest of your life. Sometimes an unfulfilled space in your heart's energy is filled by a pet that completes your inner being during their time with you.

Others teach their guardian an important Karmic lesson they need to learn. An example: A puppy ran out into the road and was killed. The owner learned to NEVER allow pets near a road. After that the pet chose to return to share happy times with his owner. See ***

Some animals have a heroic task to complete such as the bomb sniffing dog that was killed while saving a platoon of servicemen and women, or a dog that retrieved a child from drowning in a pool, or a cat that saved its family from a fire.

If the guardian, individuals or humanity does **not** "get" the lesson or purpose for their being, then that God Animal will reincarnate again and endure the exact same scenario until the lesson recipient understands and changes their behavior.

God Animals also have a social awareness for the greater good of the animal kingdom and all species, or a cathartic lesson to teach humanity. Neglected and abused animals that you find in homeless shelters that are euthanized or hoarding breeders who keep animals living in horrific and other heinous conditions, dog fighting victims, any animal that is a "victim" of an abhorrent cause, event or activity, all, are probably God Animals that have volunteered to help change conditions.

The horses in Central Park that became overheated in the midday summer city climate changed the conditions for other equines. New laws were passed to protect the horses and correct those conditions.

The dolphins that were caught in fishing nets or beached whales led the way to reform and solutions that bettered the lives for all animals that followed.

Animal extinction, abuse and cruelty cases, elephants hunted for their ivory, think about something horrific and it's probably God Animals doing their job! God bless them!

Brent Atwater's
Just Plain Love® Books presents

God Animals also assist from a Universal plane after they have crossed over by channeling pertinent information to their humans. Some assist pets on the other side by helping in Pet Heaven. Others are instrumental in instructing or influencing their person's purpose on earth. An example: After a dog dies, their guardian is led to foster and find homes for unloved pets.

God Animals and Reincarnation
People who experience a God Animal, understand that VERY special level of connection that is even above and beyond a soul connected pet. They are often disappointed to learn their pet is not returning in their **present** lifetime because its job is complete. To return again in the current lifetime would interfere with the overall inter connectiveness of the lesson that God Animal came to teach.

   However, just because your God Animal is not returning does not mean it will not accompany you in **another** lifetime. At the point of newfound wisdom*** sometimes your God Animal may choose at its discretion to return for happier times. Others may have "signed on" for later incarnation learning opportunities!

What do I do since my God Animal is not returning in this lifetime?
Many years of communicating with animals document a reoccurring pattern. God Animals usually send another pet to be with their former guardian. Why? God Animals "over soul" new pets to continue participating in and keeping a watchful presence over their "person."

Sometimes a God Animal will not come back to their initial person but to another individual in that specific lifetime.

In the middle of the night Caleb stood by Diana's bedside staring at her and telepathically awakening her. The house was on fire! He saved her family.

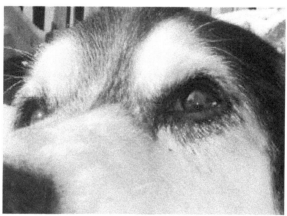

In our Reading Caleb was not going to return to Diana. His Soul's assignment was to be with her Family. Caleb showed me that he is returning to be with her daughter when she is 14 years old and to be with her blonde haired blue eyed grandchild when she is 6 to 8 years old. As a God Animal, Caleb's soul's assignment is Diana's family unit and not her.

Do God Animals and regular pets have a spiritual awareness?
In my opinion, the very fact that pets DO reincarnate indicates a spiritual awareness of their soul's contract with their human guardian. Animals survive on their keen instincts, highly evolved senses and intuition that create their level of consciousness. They operate

completely in present awareness.

Animals act from their whole consciousness and comprehend beyond the bounds of known reality.

Many owners and pets read each other's mind and communicate telepathically on a regular basis which is considered a "spiritual" awareness interchange. Some can sense unseen "energy" intrusions like the Seizure dogs or Cancer sniffing pets. What about the cat that can smell death energy? How often have you watched and trusted your pet's reaction to a new friend or situation?

Being aware of and living in "all there is," is a major component of spiritual awareness and animals are masters!

Guardian Angels Can Take a Pet Form

A Guardian Angel who chose a Beagle's form to watch over its person is one of the most interesting readings I've done in 20 years of consultations!

When I first tried to "see" Blanche's energy, I was unable to find it! That has NEVER happened to me! After multiple attempts, I told the owner that we could reschedule to see if she would appear another day OR I'd refund her money.

Minutes after I said that, I looked at the photo again, and an "energy being" started communicating with me. Still no energy form to look at. So I asked "show me your energy" and an Angel appeared. No wonder- I was look ing for a dog's energy. Needless to say the Angel's story was fascinating as to "why" she had chosen this Beagle body to watch over her person and all of the other information she provided my client! Although rare, God's Angels can "take on the form" of an animal for their Earthly assignment! See YTube video on Blanche's Reading.

Reincarnation can occur 3 Ways

There are three processes that an animal can use for reincarnation.

1. The "Walk in" contract.
This occurs when the deceased pet's energy
    MOVES INTO ANOTHER pet's body
    that is ALREADY on earth
    whose soul has AGREED TO RELOCATE
    WHEN the departed pet's energy RETURNs.

Can the new puppy or a mature animal that was born BEFORE my pet died, be my reincarnated animal?
YES! At times your pet's new body will arrive on earth before your pet's old body passes away.
    A **"walk-in"** is a <u>pre-</u>arranged soul agreement (made in Heaven) between your original pet's spirit and the "delivery soul."

Brent Atwater's
Just Plain Love® Books presents

After your pet's soul departs his old physical body, he "**walks into" (i.e. transfers his life force energy)** the "new body" that was created and delivered to await his return. The delivery pet having completed what he wanted to accomplish on earth is ready to go back across the veils. So we have a perfectly good body ready to be occupied by the pet that passed.

As your pet enters his new vehicle, the "delivery soul" (like an auto company's driver delivering a new car) then returns to Heaven (the manufacturer), having completed his "delivery" job of bringing a new body onto earth.

Sometimes the delivery body can arrive years or days in advance. That's how an older pet or a newborn puppy can become your "new" reincarnate.

The "walk-in" transition process can occur immediately in a newborn, overnight or over a few months' time. It is all determined by the animals' spiritual arrangement.

Usually the "walk in" contract takes several weeks to complete. It's like refurbishing a car. The life force electromagnetics of the deceased pet has to be rewired into the new body. The delivery pet's "wiring" has to be removed so he can go back to Heaven.

This type of exchange oftentimes occurs during a prolonged illness or other timeframes that would necessitate the pet's body to rest and sleep a lot which allows the Universe to accomplish the rewiring. As each day passes you will recognize your old pet's characteristics appearing more and more until the process is finished. It's a win win situation for both souls!

The best example of this "walk in" process is about Rinna now Darby and Austin's now Carbon's story in *"I'm Home!" a Dog's Never Ending Love Story.*

FYI, human "walk-ins" have many websites that can further define and explain this process.

What does the energy of a "walk in" animal look like?

First you watch an animal's life force energy cross over the death line and reassemble into sparkler form. At that point, a normal reincarnation would recoagulate their energy in a future timeline. However a "walk in's" energy does an immediate U turn. It goes back over the death line into the previous life energy and not into future energy.

Why, because the host body is back in the pre death environment of the original pet. It's very interesting to watch! Then I describe the body that the pet's Soul has inhabited so you will know "where your pet went." ☺

Tic Toc (on the right) passed on November 12th. The delivery body arrived many years before their walk in contract actually occurred. Andy (on the left) was adopted November 17. At that time, their Mom knew something was "very familiar" yet didn't realize Andy was the return of Tic Toc. As you can see from the eyes this is a very intense soul.

2. "Soul Braiding" is another process of reincarnation.

"Soul braiding" is a **shared** body contract. It occurs when the deceased pet returns as a roommate within a living pet's body. (Move over Rover ☺)

Do you mean that two pet souls can occupy one body?
Yes. **A "soul braid"** occurs when a deceased pet's spirit moves into a living pet's body and blends with their energy. The current pet then acts like and has characteristics of **both** animals. Think of it this way, 2 pet soul roommates living inside one body!

Due to the integration process, a "soul braid," takes more time due to the rearrangement of the two life force energies into one body and personality! It's like taking 2 cars and rewiring them into one!

Often the living pet will appear to have an illness for a period of time. That's when the process of interweaving the electromagnetics of two soul frequencies occurs.

When the living pet "gets well," it will display BOTH of the pet's characteristics. Miss Sisi (on the right), moved her soul into Miss Angel (on the left) to stay with her beloved Victoria Ford longer.

In the "walk-in" and "soul-braid" scenarios, your heart will understand and inherently know which process is transpiring as your past pet continues to emerge. With either process, YOU have your pet back!

3. The simplest most prevalent type of reincarnation is a new body.

That's when your deceased pet's energy returns in a new physical form. Think of it as putting on a new outfit, same energy different suit.

Animal Life after Death & Animal Reincarnation
Everything You Always Wanted to Know!

How long does the reincarnation process take?
There are times when your pet may attempt several different entrances BEFORE they get just the right body and circumstance to come back home to you. Ollie's story is a purrfect example ☺

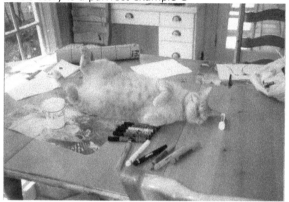

Your pet's return can be as short as several hours or take place many years later. Be patient with whatever re-entry timeframe they require to acquire that new body OR the process that has been chosen in order to return to you. Sometimes your childhood pet doesn't return until you are an adult. Your souls' contracts determine the how, what, where and when.

Brent Atwater's
Just Plain Love® Books presents

Can my animal reincarnate into another form?
A pet will select the **most appropriate animal form** to accompany you during the particular life phase that you will be sharing together.

Your pet can reincarnate as male or female or as a different breed of the same or another species.

That lop-eared bunny or squirrel you had as a child may choose to return as your female "tigger kitty," your favorite ferret, then a Great Dane and later as your horse when you're an adult or a parakeet when you're in assisted living. Be open minded. Do not expect the exact same physical image or gender. Your pet will determine how best to be there with you.

How do pets know what bodies they have to choose from?
Most pets will usually reincarnate within the same species and with your animal preferences. After all, they know you well! As stated before, animals will choose **the most appropriate form** for the specific time and environmental factors in your life when they return to you.

Can a Pet choose to delay or speed up the timing of his return?
Yes. If your pet sees negative energy and dissention in your environment, life obstacles that you need to move through or Karmic lessons that you have to complete before he comes back, he'll wait if those factors are not resolved. If you are experiencing emotional or physical events within your life or family that are not in your contract, she'll wait.

If a reading predicted a specific timeframe, there CAN be multiple inappropriate events, emotions, environmental and health factors that can cause your pet to hesitate till all "the situations" settle down, are cleared up and or completed. SO if your pet is slow in coming back, analyze your life and lifestyle to see what you need to fix!

On the other hand, if a pet determines that all the Universal circumstances and conditions are right, they may "come on down" earlier!

My life is difficult right now. Can I renegotiate our contract?
As mentioned earlier, if you don't want to subject your pet to personal hardships, you **can** renegotiate a soul agreement. Soul contracts are usually made "on

the other side" before birth. Due to the "free will choice" factor, they are flexible which creates a rescindable element to your initial negotiations.

It's possible that even your best intentions were not feasible once you arrived and faced Earth reality. So you **can** opt out

At some point in eternity, in some incarnation its best to honor that contract in order to continue the learning path that you chose to accomplish together.

If a pet's reincarnation contracts are finished can he still come back?
A pet that is an **old soul** has been here many times. If he has completed his spiritual evolution and agreements with you, that old soul does not have to return in any incarnations.

An old soul pet can <u>choose</u> to reincarnate just for the fun of it if he wants to accompany you further.

More often than not, an old soul pet will lead you to and be the "over soul" i.e. the guiding essence for a new pet rather than returning.

Can a pet wait around until you to choose a body for him and then take possession of that body?
NO. Some folks will say go pick a body and then the soul will enter. NOT! That is a way of placating clients because the "reader" can't get the information needed or determine and see what is happening in the future for your pet. It's an easy way out for them.

Reincarnation is a soul and energy contract. You and your pet have already set up exactly how this will occur before you came to earth. You do not choose his body. According to laws of physics, you can't choose what his frequency vibration is attuned to, even though you are able to sense his energy. The animal must choose the energy that he will inhabit and resonate with. His choice is made BEFORE he arrives into that particular body's energy field. If the pet is a walk in, this choice would have been predetermined before his transition.

A lot of people are fooled into thinking that their pet is reincarnated because they have picked out a puppy in a litter that has been born or about to be born and magically it will have the soul of the deceased pet *because they want it to be so*! Oh so WRONG information!! The people who perpetuate that "pick a body notion" can't **see** energy!

Since you can't verify what a person perceives telepathically to tell you, some actually believe they have a reincarnated pet that is NOT any way an energy match to the original soul's energy pattern.

Also beware of the AC who states "He's at Rainbow Bridge and hasn't made up his mind yet." Or "I can tell you at a later reading." Those words mean that the AC could not access the information you want to know.

IF a pet has a soul contract with you that agreement was made BEFORE you came on Earth. Therefore that information IS available **at any time** to someone who can connect to the correct frequency.

There is plenty of food, water and sunshine.

Many people consult an average of 3 to 5 animal communicators. However it's not necessary to have more than one reading about reincarnation. Why? Because any and all information you want to know is in your pet's energy field whether alive, deceased or reincarnated. And you should be able to have all those answers IF your communicator can talk about your pet's reincarnation.

That's correct, you can read a pet that is alive and know if they are going to reincarnate or not. Additionally whether alive or dead, you can know when, where and what they will look like in future lives! Just look at your pet's Spirit. As the say, an (living energy) image is worth a thousand words!

When does the Pet's Spirit/ Soul enter the body it has chosen for reincarnation?

It's your pet's decision to determine when to inhabit a body in accordance with your agreement. It may enter a fetus at any time or change its mind thus creating a stillborn birth. Or it may enter the place holding "Walk –in" body immediately after death. **Your pet's choice** of timing is **always perfect**!

"Over Soul" Agreements may SEEM like a reincarnation but it's NOT!

Many pet parents are so distraught over the death of their dog, cat, horse, finned or feathered beloved companion that they think their living pet has become the deceased pet. Why? Because it's "acting like" the old pet.

A pet being "over souled" makes you think "he acts like my old pet" by displaying some recognizable characteristics. However, an "over souled" pet does **not** ignite that **deep and certain knowing** that "this IS my reincarnated pet or my old girlfriend" on an ongoing basis. With an over souled pet, you will inwardly question yourself and have some doubts.

Brent Atwater's
Just Plain Love® Books presents

That in and of itself is a **very** telling answer for your heart.

Over souling occurs when a living pet **agrees to take direction from** a deceased animal or human. Over souling is an intermittent process and NOT a permanent arrangement. The deceased pet or human's energy does NOT enter the living animal. If it did merge with the living pet it would be permanent and that process would be a "walk-in" or soul braid.

Merging with a living pet's energy on an intermittent basis would make the living animal very sick. Why? Because each visit or merge into the living pet's body would disrupt and alter the electromagnetics of the earth pet's life force energy. Accommodating the coming and goings would make the living pet very sick or likely to have seizures. Therefore over souling is done **by directives** and **not** mini merges.

The over souling process is also a way your pet can just check in to keep in touch with you, let you know they are OK and are there for you in Spirit, in addition to seeing that everything is going the way "it should be" according to their heavenly perspective.

Because you want your pet back so badly, wishful thinking on your part creates difficulty and confusion in telling whether it's a straight reincarnation or an "over soul" process. However, no matter how often the over souling occurs, the pet parent WILL eventually determine what's going on and know it's not a permanent "come back" kid.

Can a pet reincarnate as a human or vice versa?

Every living thing humans, animals, rocks, trees, water all have a specific energy pattern or electromagnetic vibrational frequency range that sustains the physical form it inhabits. Energy can easily reform at a like or lower level.

What is the difference between human energy and animal energy? A healthy human frequency has a range of 68- 72 MHz FYI; each organ in your body had a specific vibrational identity. Vibrational medicine uses this information to address, correct and reconfigure unhealthy energy patterns in a person in order to resolve health problems.

Animal energy frequencies vibrate at a lower MHz level than human energy. That does not make them a lesser being. They simply have a lower frequency pattern to sustain their biological housing.

Can a pet reincarnate as a human? After almost 20 years of research and experience, animals do not usually reincarnate in human form because an animal's biological body has a lower electromagnetic frequency range than that of a human being.

Energy is not normally able to reformulate into a higher frequency than the original spirit. However in the Yogic transmigration belief of reincarnation there are 8.4 million life times that souls evolve through from beginning to end. This process starts with a single cell's life and continues until that cell reaches the highest evolution possible which is considered to be a human form. This Yogic transmigration system also believes in due time an animal will eventually evolve into human form.

Using their transmigration theory, the Yogic belief implies that some animal souls prematurely skip several lifetimes in order to become a human before they have completed the incremental evolutionary process. This means that animal spirit moved into a

Brent Atwater's
Just Plain Love® Books presents

higher biological body before their soul had learned the necessary spiritual lessons required to be evolved into a human being. Yogic believers consider that these under evolved reincarnated souls exhibit excessive "animal like" qualities when they are in human form.

As you are reading, keep in mind to always go with your inner guidance and what resonates with **you**.

The physical body that each soul chooses to inhabit must be in a frequency range that the soul can sustain for that specific lifetime. Example: a flower can't be a human, because its soul's normal frequency range does not match the final form it wants to exist in.

Do humans come back as pets? Most pets that you might want to think is a human you once knew, is simply the process of that human's spirit over souling your pet. Though rare, there can always be exceptions to any rule.

Most humans who have evolved to the highest frequency do not want to go down to a pet's vibrational range. That's why they arrange an over soul agreement with the pet. Over souling saves a lot of electromagnetic reorganization in order to reinhabit that animal's body. Over souling occurs when a living pet agrees to take direction from a deceased animal or person.

Think about it, why would a human want to completely rewire their energy blueprint in order to fit into a lower resonance body with a shorter life span? All that person's soul has to do is create a contract with your pet to direct and influence all of the consenting animal's activities. That way your favorite person or pet, while still enjoying Heaven, is still connected to you and your daily activities.

The over soul process is much easier than being rewired. Plus it accomplishes the same outcome!

Always remember, no soul whether a cellular organism, animal or human form is greater or lesser than the other. All of their respective vibrational energy and frequency patterns are part of the Universal evolutionary process.

Animals can appear to behave like humans.
My research indicates that older deceased individuals usually "over soul" pets.

Example: a friend had a dog that mimicked a lot of the characteristics of her deceased husband.
As an "over soul," (i.e. a soul in heaven who provides guidance to an earthly being), her husband's spirit taught the dog about his wife's likes and dislikes. Among other things, she liked to be kissed goodnight and hated sharing the bathroom!

Pet Life after Death & *"I'm Home!"*

First and foremost every professional should advise you to only use the information that resonates with **your soul** BEFORE they start any consultation.

You and **ONLY you** are the **direct connection** to your pet's energy! Your soul KNOWS and resounds with what is really true!
However emotions can affect how you filter that information. Sometimes wanting a reincarnation so bad or chanting affirmations will NOT make it come true nor is it in the highest and best good for either you or your pet.

Ways to communicate with your deceased pet:
Meditate and ask within your heart.
Use an animal or interspecies communicator, pet psychic, medium, intuitive or clairvoyant.
Work with an AIH practitioner.
Talk with an Animal Hope Counselor™.
Listen to your inner guidance and knowing.
Use any and all methods that "ring true" with you in any combination.
Learn to communicate directly with your pet.

What can affect communication with my pet?
When tuned into or correctly connected with your pet's frequency, one can talk to a pet's energy before during and throughout the entire death transition process AND while they are going to and living at the other side!
If the communicator/ psychic has a weak or incorrect telepathic connection with your pet's specific frequency, then circumstances and conditions

Brent Atwater's
Just Plain Love® Books presents

surrounding your pet's death may affect that animal's energy transmissions. Some very ill animals may seem to have a weak "signal" and animals involved in sudden death trauma, may also appear to take a while to transmit because they are still in shock from being on the other side. Clarity and correct information is all about a precise accurate connection.

What other things can affect communication?
Perhaps the AC neglected to ask permission to talk with the pet and is not getting 100% cooperation. He may be tuning into the wrong frequency range or misinterprets the psychic feelings from which he derives and develops his information.

Animals can also provide untruthful information just like humans. Uncooperative animals might not want to "talk" or "share." I dealt with a cat that took 2 weeks to get his permission to have a conversation with me! As his health declined he became more agreeable.

YOU or your communicator's limiting beliefs will affect a reading. Personal emotional and/or mental filters will alter the facts. Expectations placed on a reading can greatly distort the information shared and the reception of that knowledge.

Be careful about "free readings" no matter how desperate you are to connect with your pet. If an upcoming pet psychic is practicing and tells you so, then that's fair for you to understand that everything might not be correct.

Many people are jumping on the "reincarnation bandwagon." A lot of hearts are hurt, when uneducated individuals tout themselves as being able to access the information YOU want to know or identify YOUR pet as being reincarnated when in fact it has not! They may get some facts correct but are incorrect in identifying a reincarnate.

What's the difference between an animal/interspecies communicator (AC), pet psychic and AIH readings?

AC's telepathically connect (defined as Communication through means other than the normal 5 senses) with your pet while I see dead pet spirits or living energy. AC's use psychic abilities; AIHs use the physics of actual energy, i.e. the pet's spirit.

An animal intuitive, interspecies communicator or a pet psychic mentally tunes into your pet and then downloads their information. From what the AC telepathically perceives, they transform those impressons into the information you are told.

An AIH practitioner looks at your dead pet's Spirit (life force energy) to see where it has been, watches where it is currently and then looks at its position in

the future.) AIH information is obtained from actually looking at a dead pet's spirit (life force energy) and watching their activity while talking with that animal's spirit throughout all realms of time.
AIHs can describe what your new pet will look like by looking at them!
Animals can NOT communicate "untruthful information" to an AIH practitioner because what they see is what you get! Your pet's spirit/energy picture is worth a gazillion words and tons of information.

   Both types of readings contribute invaluable yet different and complementary perspectives that can help you access, validate and understand what your pet is doing.

Is contacting my pet all the time selfish?
As each other's "true love," keeping in touch is not an invasion of privacy. **However** you should ask permission to tap into your pet's energy field each time you want to access it. Your pet may choose to honor your request or they can say not now, later! FYI, when an animal has just come back to earth,

you're aware of this fact and want to talk with them, try to curb that urge. A newly arrived pet needs a little time to acclimate to the earth's environment and to their new body.

How to Bring Your Pet's Energy to Earth

You are waiting for me aren't you?

I'm coming BACK from Rainbow Bridge to be with you - AGAIN!

First, protect you! Why? When you open a connection to the other side, you *only* want your pet to respond. Then you won't be a portal for **all** energies that want to communicate with someone on earth.

Protecting yourself requires getting your prayers and intent on a specific tract. Let's look at how to pray in order to carefully craft and direct your prayers.

Brent Atwater's
Just Plain Love® Books presents

How to Pray: Be SPECIFIC!

The Universe lives in forever time and your leased vehicle (body) lives in finite time, so you need to be very specific. Say:

I ASK: "ask and ye shall receive." It's a Universal Law that all those in charge of your soul's contract must respond. You're asking all those in charge of your soul to help you, now! Why not use ALL the powers you have on heaven and earth that are available to you???

It is MY INTENT (with a "T" NOT Intend) that brings your prayers into the NOW, in this incarnation, at this very moment in time. YOU MUST BE SPECIFIC!!!!!!!!!!!!!!

They live in "forever" time and in "all that is," so be VERY specific about exactly what you want and in the VERY SPECIFIC timeframe of what you want. Not being specific (intend) is never never land, or "which incarnation?" etc. to those on the other side.

I suggest that you say your prayer 3 times. 3 is the universal number.
* The first time sets your free will to ask for help,
* the second time your prayer creates intent
* the third time to me, means you're really focused on getting this done!

Use the words Now, Forevermore and Always.
"Now," brings your prayer into the now, i.e. present. The Universe operates in a timeless forever and to have Them respond to your command you must state "now", otherwise your guides will be asking "in which incarnation, past life or parallel life do you want this done?"

"Forevermore," takes the prayer into all energy realms, incarnations and time frames. **Always,"** makes the prayer results continuous with no time lapses.

At the finale of your request Say: So be it, it is done. Thank you. "So be it," brings the prayer into the present life situation. "It is done," manifests that the prayer has become and IS a reality, NOW!

First, Take off your shoes and say your Protection Prayer
*** **Prayer for all encompassing Protection: Say: I ask and it is my intent, to surround myself in a seamless mirrored--(bubble or cocoon) of the Christ White Light (or whomever is your Higher Power), to protect me now, forevermore and always. Only allow the energy or entities which are for my soul's highest and best good to come thru. So be it, it is done. Thank you.**

If you don't do anything else, this is what you say at any time in any place, whenever you want to protect yourself!

Why do I use the words seamless and mirrored?
Seamless means nothing comes in or out unless you allow it. The concept of mirrored means that any negative energy or entity, event or whatever that is aimed at you, reflects back to the sender so that you will not be drained or affected. SO easy!

*** **If you change the wording of a prayer you will receive different results**. ***

Brent Atwater's
Just Plain Love® Books presents

We did a radio show on "Animal Communication gone wrong" on Pet Life Radio.com, that's when I decided to add this information.

Next, ask your pet's permission to work with them. Telepathically ask with your mind or heart. You will hear the answer in your inner consciousness. Now you're prepared to request your pet's energy to come to visit, contact or connect with you.
(Remember, **Do NOT use IntenD**) use **Intent**- this is a MAJOR common mistake that causes disconnection.)
FYI- Practice about 30 minutes a day. It works!
State:
I ask and it is my **intent** to contact the energy previously known as _____,
so that I can feel him here now.
I ask _____ to put your paw (nose, head, whatever) into my _____hand now.
(Use the hand that you do NOT write with, that's your "receiving energy" hand.)
SO be it. It is done. Thank you.

You can use this prayer for asking to see him in my dreams if you're uncomfortable feeling their presence.

I say this prayer 3 times to create intent, focus and clarity. Use these **exact** words. They protect you from having unwanted energies or entities visit.
IF you are **extremely** emotional at this point in time you will not be able to sense them. *Excess grief will cause disconnection as will anger and disbelief.*

Take the time to calm down! This method works! My Mother's 86 year old Garden Club members were able to do this.

What you will feel is tingles in your hand, or "thick weighty" air, a sense of pressure or cold or maybe a warm air area that is **different from** the surrounding air.

If it doesn't work at first, wait and try again. If it works the first time and then not again, ask YOURSELF what are YOU doing to block the energy. Once you have accessed their energy, it is always available to you until they start returning "home." Sometimes it takes up to 2 weeks until your pet will respond because their energy resides in eternity.

Various research materials suggest that you "contact" spirits (this works with people too!) at the same time each day for quicker results.

FYI, you can also set your intent and ask to see and or communicate with a pet in your dreams. **If** you want your pet to answer questions in your dreams, **be very specific about what you are requesting.**

You're probably wondering:
1. Now that my pet's energy is visiting me, what do I do?
   Enjoy your new awareness and your pet!
2. If I contact my animal's spirit, am I interrupting him from whatever they are supposed to be doing on the other side? NO!
3. FYI- Sometimes an animal will just "show up" to "check in you" to let you know they're OK.

Although AC or AIH sessions contribute greatly to peace of mind and help you understand the decisions you made were the "right thing to do" during the events surrounding your pet's death, they also provide comfort by communicating with your pet. This continues your loving, close connection and "covers

Brent Atwater's
Just Plain Love® Books presents

you with a warm hug" which makes everything a little less traumatic.

However, ask yourself the questions below:
Are you being obsessive about contacting your pet because you feel you can't move on?
Are you SO upset and consumed by sorrow that you are unrealistically lonely?
Are you so co-dependent that you can't let go?

Even though you miss your pet terribly, there is a time to seek awareness and a time to move forward. **It's unhealthy for any individual to stay stuck in negative grief**.

"I can't get over this" attitudes are unhealthy for your animal's spiritual energy.
1. **It will limit their visits**
2. Slow down signs to let you know they are OK
3. Can **harm** your pet's long-term transition to a higher realm or back to you.

Be aware that there will be a time when your pet will no longer respond to your request because he has moved on to a higher plane or is reformulating to come back or readapting to being on earth.

For example, Mike came to visit me on multiple occasions including birthdays and anniversaries. After several years he no longer appeared. Inherently I knew he had ascended into another spiritual realm and a higher purpose. And yes, I still miss his physical presence.

*** Practice all exercises about 30 minutes per day for at least 2 weeks to begin with or until your pet responds on a regular and when you request basis.

How to Touch Your Deceased Pet's Energy

Before Mike died, I did not know feeling energy "on the other side" was even possible! I'd heard about it, but blew it off as "airy Fairy." Plus, I was raised as a Christian and was really afraid to be involved in anything "like that!"

From the other side, Mike patiently instructed me how to do this process. After I learned, we would hold hands when I was afraid and he would kiss me every night before I went to sleep. He slept beside me for months *after* he had vacated his biological being.

Growing up I always heard that "God is Love." After my experiences and learning what I'm going to teach you, I **totally** understand! I KNOW beyond a shadow of a doubt that energy and love is forever and always --alive and well and **NEVER ending!**

When your pet has responded to your request to be present in "energy or steam form" or "Spirit" form on earth, you'll sense their presence.

Brent Atwater's
Just Plain Love® Books presents

Now it's time to "touch" your pet.

1. Rub your hands together until they are warm in order to activate the nerve endings in your palms and fingertips so you can sense energy to the "max." If you need to "refresh" your sensory sensitivity, just do this "warming up" exercise and start over as many times as necessary.

2. spread your fingers apart with about -at least- a half inch of space between each finger, like a wide toothed comb. That increases your sensitivity to feeling energy.

3. **Very** SOFTLY**, as if you are trying to touch the dust on butterfly wings,** start SLOWLY sweeping your hands horizontally back and forth within about a 4 foot wide path within a 4 foot high rectangular area in the vicinity you sense your pet is located.

Continuously scan for their energy back and forth left to right or vice versa and top to bottom through that space. (Demonstration on our YouTube channel)

Keep working in rectangular quadrants until you feel and or sense "something" in the manner that YOUR body registers/ receives energy input.

It can feel like:
a thicker, puffier, denser, usually cooler area or a section that causes your hand to tingle.

It can also feel like "fat air", a warm ball or like two magnets pushing against one another between your hands. That's your pet! Your heart will KNOW it's them!

Being "sensitive to a different feel of air" is how you progress. When you get really good at this, you can learn to feel the edges of their form, even all their "feetsies" or feathers! If you get REALLY good, you can feel their whiskers.

This may take some time time getting used to. Your reward is worth it!

* Don't get frustrated, in time, this works. On my YouTube Channel, we have Videos demonstrating this and other techniques.

*** The softer and more consistent your movements are and the **slower** (i.e. don't rush this) you approach *any* energy field, **the greater** the sensory input you receive.

Be patient and **practice, practice, practice!** This will allow your tactile recognition to occur more rapidly.

One of my clients would get her cat to lie around her shoulders.   She also would have him put his paw in her hand on command. You can even feel your animal kiss you, bump into you with that ball you should be throwing or sleeping next to you each night!!!

Important note: If your animal is regrouping his energy to come back and you're doing this exercise, his energy field will be thinner as time grows closer for his return. Rather than being disappointed, focus on the fact that soon you'll be petting them in the flesh!

Brent Atwater's
Just Plain Love® Books presents

What's the importance of this exercise?
Once you have learned to feel, connect and resonate with your pet's energy, you will be more "in tune" with what your pet "feels like."

This knowledge allows you to be more sensitive to their progress. You'll be able to "feel" them getting closer. Like birth contractions, you may feel waves of their energy building more and more as they come closer. These waves will provide compelling and undeniable guidance that will lead you to your pet.

You'll be able to sense when they leave the purple energy veils of life after death and begin transition into their red life force energy field. If you are energy sensitive, you may even know the moment your pet comes back on earth.

When I am looking at, watching and tracking energy, it's extremely interesting to see a pet's energy turn into a fetus and takes on its new life form within the mother's womb.

When your pet is born or takes full possession of a "walk in" vehicle or participates in the "soul braid" process; your heart will "feel them." There is NO way you will misinterpret your inner urgings to find them and not know where they are. You'll "feel it!"

It's a KNOWING that is irrefutable!

*Death is the Beginning
of your New Life together!*
Animal Life after Death and Reincarnation is Real!

Animal Life after Death Book by Brent Atwater

Can I use this exercise to locate a lost pet?

Yes, but in a different way!
Once you learn to recognize your pet's energy in your heart and personal energy field, here are 2 techniques to locate a pet:

Brent Atwater's
Just Plain Love® Books presents

1. Say: I ask and it is my intent to find _____
now. Then stand very quietly and undistracted.
Say: _Pet's name_____ from the love in my heart,
I send you my energy to follow safely home to me.
Come home to me now. Thank you.
This creates an energy path for your animal to sense
its way back. Numerous TV stories feature animals
that travel across country or found their guardians
years after they were lost!

2. Say: I ask and it's my internet to find _____
now. _____ lead me to where you are now!
Lead me to where you are now! So be it it is done!

Then stand very still and like the second hand of a
clock, **SLOWLY** rotate your body until you feel a pull in
your energy field. Then walk toward that direction
until it stops.

When the "energy pulling" feeling stops, then start all
over and repeat this process until you find your
beloved pet or any animal you are searching for.

Even a deceased pet's energy can be found this way.
I learned this when the Cable man ran over my white
Persian kitten named Kisses and threw her in the
woods. I knew being deaf, she would never run
away. So I kept saying this prayer and using this
technique until I found her.

Doreen Virtue advises that you ask your animal's
guardian Angels to tell your pet to come home to you
now! Whatever method you use, be sure to add
safely and thank you at the end of each request.

How do I see my pet's Aura and "Steam" or Spirit form?

and yes they will look like steam.

Step 1: Use the previous technique to ask your deceased pet's energy to show up on Earth. State: I ask and it is my **intent** to <u>contact</u> the energy previously known as _____,
so that I can feel him here now.

Brent Atwater's
Just Plain Love® Books presents

Step 2: Once your deceased pet has responded and you have located and can feel their energy presence, then state:

1. I ask and it is my intent to see my deceased _pet name_ energy now, I ask and it is my intent to see my deceased __pet name ___energy now, I ask and it is my intent to see my deceased ___pet's name__) energy now.

2. Then close your eyes tight and say "shift energy and refocus now."

3. Open your eyes softly, try not to blink. Call you pet by saying
_____ show yourself to me, in front of me now, show yourself to me, in front of me now, show yourself to me, in front of me now.

In time they will show up!!! Be patient. It may take 2 weeks or more but they will show up. If you have seen them out of the corner of your eye, you must specifically ask them to "show up IN FRONT OF you, so you will have a **very clear vision of them**!

Do you want your Pet to provide more information?
When your pet has taken the time to reformulate their energy on earth for you to see them, whether out of the corner of your eye or across the room, it's an opportune time to ask for more information.

I often saw Possum Kitty running from room to room and Hairy kitty's steam sleeping in my open office drawer. Sometimes I see my yellow lab "Boo Bear" running across the golf course with his ball, to show me he's happy. Yes, you will be able to do this!

Ask them to show you more.
Say: "__Pet's name_ show me what I need to know about you now."
YOU can also say while they are making their steam appearance:
"tell me what you want me to know <u>now</u>"

(Remember repeating each phrase 3 times makes it REAL clear!) Then listen to what you hear in your heart.
Be sure to thank your pet for coming.
I'd also invite them to return anytime those chose to do so!

Brent Atwater's
Just Plain Love® Books presents

What can prohibit my pet from visiting me?
Anger, disbelief, crying, excess grief and guilt limit an animal's ability to use his energy to communicate, contact and come into your consciousness. When you're less upset, you'll have greater clarity for the subliminal signs and nuances that you may be missing.

After Mike was killed, he would begin to formulate in glitterized sparkly spirit steam form in front of me. I was so emotionally traumatized that I couldn't handle it! And so scared that when he asked to show up for me to see him, I wouldn't allow him to do so.

It is my **greatest** regret that I did not allow Mike to present himself as a living energy being, while he was in an energy state capable of assembling into a recognizable form. Many individuals have seen their beloved deceased people or pets' energy form during a visit. To them it was very comforting and healing. There is nothing to fear and a great deal to learn "face to face." All processes of connection and communication are the same with humans or animals.

Remember practice makes perfect!!!
It will take a while for you to get used to allowing and accessing another frequency.   Try to practice about 30 minutes each day, without shoes and when you are rested. You CAN do this!

Can other Pets that I had in my past come visit me? Yes! Any animal or living energy being on the other side can choose to visit at any time as an individual or in a group!

Memorials, Grave sites and Altars

Some people create memorials, grave sites or altars with candles, flowers, photos and keepsake momentos. Others freeze dry or have a taxidermist preserve their pet. Many folks have their animals ashes incorporated into artwork or made into a bracelet, crystal or another remembrance object.

Then the pet parent goes to that physical location or mentally visualizes a connection with their pet thru a specific "memorial form." If this is your choice, be SURE that you are not clinging to what WAS by believing and limiting your pet's essence to **that specific location**. Don't focus on their "deadness."

If YOU believe you can only have a connection with your pet at that memorial area, freeze dried body or keepsake piece, your animal will honor your choices. **Your attitude about them having a specific location ONLY at your memorial** will limit their signs, connection and slow down reincarnation.
*** **A Pet's "sparkler form" energy and their Love is ALIVE and can be with you ALL the TIME, EVERYWHERE!**

When you choose to believe deceased pet's Souls are *living energy* and *can be anywhere and everywhere,* **only then** can they honor their agreement to "come back to you."

The Rainbow Bridge Poem is ONLY ½ the Story!

His Soul begins the search for the Haven of your heart.

The original Rainbow Bridge poem was written by an unknown author many years ago, this universal Pet Loss poem tells only half of the story!

If you believe in pet life after death and Reincarnation like I do, that Rainbow Bridge poem represents a dead end (literally) for your pet. It states their soul never evolves- it just dies and YOU have to die to join them! WRONG! from a spiritual point of view.

I wrote and created the Return from Rainbow Bridge series to represent those of us that believe in our pets never ending love and ability to **Return from Rainbow Bridge.**

Brent Atwater's
Just Plain Love® Books presents

I believe my **Poems** and **Videos** tell the **whole story** and embrace the eternal cycle of life,   See the Return from Rainbow Bridge information section at the end of this book.

I have created Poems for Dogs, Cats, Horses, Rescue and Special Needs Pets and one for all animals in general.

Both the Poems and Videos are translated into multiple languages so you can help heal hearts by passing them forward or sharing with a friend. You can always download a copy of each Poem in your language or for your specific type of pet from Brent's website, Facebook Page or Group or from our Pet reincarnation Blog. Videos of the Poem are on Brent Atwater's YouTube Channel.

Does your Soul think your Pet is coming back
from Rainbow Bridge?
NO, you are NOT "crazy"!!!
Pet Reincarnation is Real

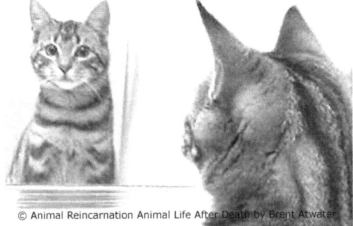

© Animal Reincarnation Animal Life After Death by Brent Atwater

Animal Life after Death & Animal Reincarnation
Everything You Always Wanted to Know!

Return from Rainbow Bridge

When an Animal dies his Soul transitions to a special place in Heaven
called the Rainbow Bridge.
There He is alive and well, a part of Never Ending Love.
He is healed, whole and restored.

He meets special friends, family and loved ones. They run and play together.
There is plenty of food, water and sunshine.
Everyone is warm, safe and comfortable.

He visits you in dreams with memories of the special times you shared.
He is happy and content, EXCEPT for one thing.
He misses that special bond with the person he had to leave behind.
He sends signs to let you know he is thinking about and watching over you.
His Soul is ALWAYS by your side.
He has NEVER stopped loving you!

Then the day comes when your Pet wants to be back.
There are promises to keep.
He quivers and sparkles with intent.
It's time to return to Earth as you both have agreed.
His energy vibrates faster and faster,
forming a Heart to be loved.

He feels the pull of your prayers and yearning.
He is strenghtened by the power of your belief in Never Ending Love.
Full of Hope and Faith he leaves the safety of Rainbow Bridge.
His Soul begins the search for the Haven of your heart.

In perfect timing that moment arrives.
You find one another!
Time stands still as you look into each other's Soul.

Your heart is etched with the feeling of recognition.
Cautiously you move forward filling the gaps to complete your bond.
As you look into trusting eyes, your touch caresses his beloved head.
All sadness is gone.
Your heart is whole again!

Your Pet has returned from the Rainbow Bridge.
Together you begin another journey
in the Eternal Cycle of Life!
Your Love is here
Now,
Forever and Always!

*****

Author: Brent Atwater

From Ms. Atwater's book Animal Reincarnation:
Animal Life after Death- Everything You Always Wanted to Know!
www.JustPlainLoveBooks.com   www.BrentAtwater.com

Brent Atwater's
Just Plain Love® Books presents

a Dog's Return from Rainbow Bridge

When a Dog dies his Soul transitions to a special place in Heaven
called the Rainbow Bridge.
There He is alive and well, a part of Never Ending Love.
He is healed, whole, and restored.

He sniffs special friends, meets family and hugs loved ones.
They chase one another, play and bark together.
There is plenty of food, treats, chewies, balls, bones and sunshine.
Everyone is warm, safe and comfortable in their beds.

He visits you in dreams with memories of the special times you shared.
He is happy and content EXCEPT for one thing.
He misses that special bond with the person he had to leave behind.
He sends signs to let you know he is thinking about and watching over you.
His Soul is ALWAYS by your side.
He has NEVER stopped loving you!

Then the day comes when your Dog wants to be back.
There are promises to keep.
He wiggles and sparkles with intent.
It's time to return to Earth as you both have agreed.
His energy vibrates faster and faster,
forming a Heart to be loved.

He feels the pull of your Prayers and yearnings.
He is strengthened by the power of your belief in Never Ending Love.
Full of Hope and Faith he leaves the safety of Rainbow Bridge.
His Soul begins the search for the Haven of your heart.

In perfect timing that moment arrives.
You find one another!
Time stands still as you look into each other's Soul.

Your heart is etched with the feeling of recognition in his eyes.
Cautiously you move forward filling the gaps that complete your bond.
Your touch caresses his beloved velvet head.
All sadness is gone.
Your heart is whole again!

Your Dog has returned from the Rainbow Bridge.
Together you begin again,
another journey
in the Eternal Cycle of Life!
**Your Love is here
Now,
Forever and Always!**

Author: Brent Atwater
*****
Taken from Ms. Atwater's book Animal Reincarnation: Animal Life after Death-
Everything You Always Wanted to Know! Video also available
Translated into many languages
5/5/13

Animal Life after Death & Animal Reincarnation
Everything You Always Wanted to Know!

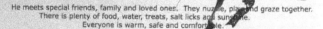

Return from Rainbow Bridge for Horses

When a Horse dies his Soul transitions to a special place in Heaven
called the Rainbow Bridge.
There He is alive and well, a part of Never Ending Love.
He is healed, whole, sound and restored.

He meets special friends, family and loved ones. They nuzzle, play and graze together.
There is plenty of food, water, treats, salt licks and sunshine.
Everyone is warm, safe and comfortable.

He visits you in dreams with memories of the special times you shared.
He is happy and content EXCEPT for one thing.
He misses that special bond with the person he had to leave behind.
He sends signs to let you know he is thinking about and watching over you.
His Soul is ALWAYS by your side.
He has NEVER stopped loving you!

Then the day comes when your Horse wants to be back.
There are promises to keep.
He neighs, paws, snorts then quivers with intent.
It's time to return to Earth as you both have agreed.
His energy vibrates faster and faster,
forming a Heart to be loved.

He feels the pull of your Prayers and yearnings.
He is strengthened by the power of your belief in Never Ending Love.
Full of Hope and Faith he leaves the safety of Rainbow Bridge.
His Soul races to search for the Haven of your heart.

In perfect timing that moment arrives.
You find one another!
Time stands still as you look into each other's Soul.

Your heart is etched with the feeling of recognition and familiarity.
Cautiously you move forward filling the gaps that complete your bond.
As you look into large trusting eyes, feeling his warm breath on your face
your touch caresses his beloved head and hugs his silken neck.
All sadness is gone.
Your heart is whole again!

Your Horse has returned from the Rainbow Bridge.
Together you begin again,
another journey
in the Eternal Cycle of Life!
Your Love is here
Now,
Forever and Always!

Author: Brent Atwater
*****
Taken from Ms. Atwater's book Animal Reincarnation: Animal Life after Death-
Answers for all your heart's Questions!
10/10/12

Brent Atwater's
Just Plain Love® Books presents

Return from Rainbow Bridge for Cats

When a Cat dies his Soul transitions to a special place in Heaven
called the Rainbow Bridge.
There He is alive and well, a part of Never Ending Love.
He is healed, whole, and restored to purrfection.

He meets special friends and head bumps loved ones.
They run, play, clean and cuddle together.
There is plenty of food, water and sunshine.
Everyone is warm, safe and comfortable.

He visits you in dreams with memories of the special times you shared.
He is happy and content EXCEPT for one thing.
He misses that special bond with the person he had to leave behind.
He sends signs to let you know he is thinking about and watching over you.
His Soul is ALWAYS by your side.
He has NEVER stopped loving you!

Then the day comes when your Cat wants to be back.
There are promises to keep.
He quivers and sparkles with intent.
It's time to return to Earth as you both have agreed.
His energy vibrates faster and faster,
forming a Heart to be loved.

He feels the pull of your Prayers and yearnings.
He is strengthened by the power of your belief in Never Ending Love.
Full of Hope and Faith he leaves the safety of Rainbow Bridge.
His Soul begins the search for the Haven of your heart.

In perfect timing that moment arrives.
You find one another!
Time stands still as you look into each other's Soul.

Your heart is etched with the feeling of recognition in his eyes.
Cautiously you move forward filling the gaps that complete your bond.
Your touch caresses his beloved velvet head.
All sadness is gone.
Your heart is whole again!

Your Cat has returned from the Rainbow Bridge.
Together you begin again,
another journey
in the Eternal Cycle of Life!
Your Love is here
Now,
Forever and Always!

Author: Brent Atwater
★★★★★
Taken from Ms. Atwater's book Animal Reincarnation: Animal Life after Death
Everything You Always Wanted to Know! Video also available
Translated into many languages
5/5/13

Animal Life after Death & Animal Reincarnation
Everything You Always Wanted to Know!

A Shelter Pet's Return from Rainbow Bridge

My heart is warm and my spirit bold
I'll never have the chance to grow old.
Depressed and scared, no matter my age
I've been put in a death row cage

I've done my best to win your attention
now left behind in loveless detention
Abused, abandoned and soon I'll die
I didn't get adopted or rescued– Why?

Was I not pretty or healthy enough
Can't you see beyond that stuff?
Where is your help when I need you?

The gas burns my eyes and my lungs too
Killing me off from loving you

WOW! What a special place in Heaven
they call it the Rainbow Bridge.
I'm alive and well, a part of Never Ending Love.
My body is healed, whole, and restored.

Oh my! Special friends, family and loved ones are here.
There is plenty of food, toys and sunshine for me.
Everyone is warm, safe and has their own bed.

I still yearn for that special bond with my own person.
I promise,
my Soul will ALWAYS be by your side.
I'll NEVER abandon or stop loving you!

Then the day comes when
it's my time to return to Earth
Full of Faith and Love I leave the safety of Rainbow Bridge.
My Soul begins again the search for the Haven of your heart.

In perfect timing that moment arrives.
We find one another!

Everything stands still as we look into each other's Soul.
I pray that you will adopt me.
Your touch caresses my head.
Oh please oh please, pick me!
so my sadness will be gone
and my heart can be whole again!

Being wanted is FINALLY here
You're taking **ME!** I'm Homeless no more!
Together we begin as a forever family.
Now I'm Happy and LOVED!
and my Soul is at peace
in this Cycle of Eternal Life!

*****

Author: Brent Atwater
From Ms. Atwater's book Animal Reincarnation: Animal Life after Death- Everything You Always Wanted to Know!
Video also availableTranslated into many languages
12/1/13

Brent Atwater's
Just Plain Love® Books presents

A Special Need Pet's Return from Rainbow Bridge

My heart is warm and my spirit bold
will you give me a chance to grow old?
"Special" and scared, no matter my age
Please don't put me in a death row cage

How blessed I am to have you as mine.
This has to be a plan so divine
that you pray and tend my every need,
and for doing everything possible I'm grateful indeed!
Your nurturing vigilance keeps me alive
and your keeping me comforatble allows me to thrive.

The time and money you sacrifice for me
makes you an Angel it has to be!
Your extraordinary support is beyond compare
and I greatly appreciate that you're always there!

But now I must say good bye,
I've experienced unconditional love so don't you cry
Get some rest as I leave this Earth
Hold me in your heart until my rebirth.

WOW! What a special place in this Heaven
they call it the Rainbow Bridge.
I'm alive and well, a part of Never Ending Love.
My body is healed, whole, and totally restored.

Oh my! Special friends, family and loved ones are here.
There is plenty of food, toys and sunshine for me.
Everyone is warm, safe and has their own bed.

I still yearn for our special bond.
I promise,
My Soul will ALWAYS be by your side.
I'll NEVER abandon or stop loving you!

Now the day comes,
it's my time to return to Earth!
Full of Faith and Love I leave the safety of Rainbow Bridge.
My Soul begins the search for the Haven of your heart.

In perfect timing that moment arrives.
We find one another!
Time stands still as we look into each other's Soul.
Your touch caresses my head.

I pray you'll recognize my healthy new body
and listen to your heart's urgings
so my sadness is gone,
and your heart can be whole again!

Let's begin again,
this time, I'll take care of YOU!

*****
Author: Brent Atwater
from Ms. Atwater's book Animal Reincarnation: Animal Life after Death- Answers for all your Heart's Questions!
Video also available Translated into many languages
8/1/14

He is happy and content,

EXCEPT for one thing....

Rainbow Bridge Memorabilia

The Rainbow Bridge poem has also evolved to represent a pet loss haven. It's a "place to go" for all good pets. Same name sites support pet loss grief forums and message boards. These online venues encourage posting pet memorials. Many individuals honor their pet's love or pay tribute to an animal's soul, for others these memorials are healing and therapeutic celebrations or a place to feel a fond remembrance. The mindset and intent of each participant *is the key* to whether this is a negative or positive practice.

People are not aware that a memorial can potentially focus their mind to only think about the "death." Some believe that deceased pets come and go as they please and even if the person focused on the pet's death the animal will still evolve. Others believe a memorial has no influence on the pet's energy. For an animal with a reincarnation contract, all previous theories are incorrect.

Brent Atwater's
Just Plain Love® Books presents

Contrary to the popularity of this "healing memorial" as reminder of who their pet *used to be*, the common grievance practice of placing your pet's image in a photo at the Rainbow Bridge can be detrimental to your pet's **living** energy.

IF you have mentally decided and think your pet is at the Rainbow Bridge, they will honor your choice until you decide otherwise. Memorial products claiming "I'll be waiting for you," perpetuate your pet is never returning. They infer you have to die before you're reunited. IF you believe that fact or focus on that mindset, your pet will honor your choice and have to come back in another incarnation.

It's imperative to know the Rainbow Bridge is just a **stopover** on the way back to you, **NOT** a place to stay for a pet that is alive and well!

In order to be a positive participant in Rainbow Bridge memorials, choose to:
be open mind to the possibility of a pets return,
celebrate the LIVING bond and
acknowledge your pet's never ending love!

Visit their memorial with excitement, anticipation and hope, that's "GOOD grief!!!"

The BEST memorials are *alive and well* in your heart- forever and always!

Signs your pet is contacting you from the other side

First and foremost- **NO, you are <u>not</u> "crazy."**

Brent Atwater's
Just Plain Love® Books presents

Dreams: Pets visit and communicate in dreams.

See: A pet may appear as a "vision" in steam form. A deceased pet may superimpose their old image over the new reincarnate's body to insure you understand "it's me again!" A wonderful example is Union Jack in *"I'm Home!" a Dog's Never Ending Love Story"*.

Smell: Oftentimes a pet parent relates they smell their wet Labrador! Don't discount a smell it's probably another sign.

Sounds: Your pet will use sounds that are familiar to you as his sign for connection. Many times I would clearly hear Friend # 1 bark to protect me. He was making sure I was aware of something, even when everything was quiet.
You'll hear them cleaning fur or drinking water in that old familiar way. Cats will purr or meow to parents across the Rainbow Bridge.
My horse would neigh, paw, shake her head and nuzzle at her lover "Liberty Blue" (who died of colic) when he would visit her in the barn. Oftentimes, you'll hear noises of other animals playing with an "imaginary friend."

Wind Chimes: I bought a wind chime for Electra, asking her to choose the one she liked. After testing them all, I KNEW which one. Some days when there is no wind, the chimes are singing. I know she's telling me she loves me from the other side.

Travel: Many clients "feel" their pets accompanying them on trips. Is it possible? YES!!! Unencumbered by a body your pet can be anywhere at any time!

Animal Life after Death & Animal Reincarnation
Everything You Always Wanted to Know!

Butterflies are the Universal symbol of reincarnation. They may come into your home, sit on your shoulder, fly around your environment or follow you. Any butterfly symbol that comes into your life is a sign!

Feathers are often signs from your pet!

Brent Atwater's
Just Plain Love® Books presents

Songs, Music or TV: Mike always played "Time, Love and Tenderness" by Michael Bolton. Before I understood this was a sign, I wondered "why does that song come on so much?" Pets will play your favorite song anywhere any time, or the song you used to sign to them. TV commercials at night before you go to bed can be a reminder he's watching over you. Never under estimate your pet's creativity!

Feel or Sense: Individuals often feel their dogs and cats lay in their lap or jump up on the bed each night as Mary would feel Rhett Butler do.

Some pets continue to sleep with their person long after their biological body has been discarded, even right up until they begin reentry. I felt Electra my "Squirrel girl" pressing close to my side when I was extremely upset and during summer "boomies" (thunderstorms).

Photos: A pet may insert their image, an orb, or their steam form into a photo you took of something entirely different! That's another "Hello!"

Unusual Occurrences: When you are crying nonstop, praying or just wondering if your beloved "family member" is okay, sometimes your pet will cause a commotion or distraction that you **recognize in your heart** is their response to let you know that they are fine! Revel would use his energy to knock his pictures off the table when Kim was upset. He was letting her know that he was right there with her!

Pets will leave toys out that you KNOW you stored in a safe place!!

Since there are no coincidences, you'll drive down a road named after your pet (like Greta in "I'm Home!" a Cat's Never Ending Love Story") or see a building or business sign with their name, letting you know they are OK.

Maybe you'll be looking in a catalogue for animal beds and all of the samples names are your pet's name, another "Hello, I love you!"

You may get a postcard in the mail or be given a bouquet of flowers with special wording on the card that triggers your heart's knowing that it's a sign from your pet. You're probably correct!

Sometimes you'll find a feather or a penny and wonder where it came from. **Your pet's signs will be very clear and distinct. Your heart and soul WILL recognize and KNOW it's them!**

NO, you are <u>not</u> "crazy."

Brent Atwater's
Just Plain Love® Books presents

Do signs mean my pet is coming back?
If yes, your pet will provide more and more obvious and frequent notice that they are on the way!

As an animal approaches relife, the experiences outlined above will gradually stop as your pet refocuses all of their energy into reassembling for their return!

If your pet is NOT reincarnating they will just "check in" off and on for the rest of your life.

How can you tell the difference?
It's not easy. Use the prayers to ask your pet for clarity. You will hear the answer in your heart.

When your prayers are answered with a "no," the signs and incidents become more sporadic. The signs will be like an old friend's call from time to time over the years. Your heart will inherently know your pet is just checking in and not going to return.

He misses that special bond with the person he had to leave behind.

© Diane Lewis Photography

Stages of Bereavement

Grieving

Initially you are devastated and will miss your pet much deeper than a mere animal loss. You recognize a "special bond" or "heart connection" and that you were blessed to share life together. You may feel, "I lost a big part of myself when she died and I feel lost without her" or even "we aren't done yet."

Feeling "blessed," "we aren't through" or "they were a part of the very fiber of my being," "my child," "the best thing ever," "everything good in my life," and my "heart beat and breath" is your soul's recognition and understanding that **your pet has shared his soul with you**.

Even in your darkest moments of grief if your feel "I miss that bond we had," "I'm not whole without my pet," and you instinctively understand that you had and may **still have** things to learn "together."

Then reuniting may be in your future.

During the bereavement process, if you feel that you want to hold onto your pet's beds, bowl and toys, collar, even putting his fur in a jar, usually there is a deeper reason. Your inner guidance inherently knows that they will be back. Keep his/her possessions in a safe place to let him know you understand he'll return and is not forgotten.

If you can't shake off this horrific grief, do something positive to honor your pet. Raise funds in your pet's name for an animal cause, foundation, shelter, rescue group or haven! Donate food to needy groups to celebrate your companion. Volunteer. Be a foster Mom. Think of ways to exemplify and memorialize all the love you shared!

Anger

At times you may be angry due to the manner in which your pet died. The sooner you release your anger, the more receptive you are to receiving signs communication and connection. Remember the spiritual perspective: There are no coincidences in life.

Every death scenario is preplanned before you each arrive on Earth.

Grief is part of the death process. However anger and extreme prolonged grief over your animal's death **may block and stall any of your pet's contact or energy movement** back into your life- sending signs, visiting in dreams and reincarnation.

As soon as you can, celebrate the love you shared!!! Then focus on the hope that your beloved companion may be on the way back home. He/she just has to get a replacement body to keep on "keeping on" with you if that's what you contracted to do.

Brent Atwater's
Just Plain Love® Books presents

Guilt

No matter what happened surrounding the transition and death of your pet, everything was exactly as **both of you** planned for that particular time and exit point!!!

You made the right decisions, you did not give up on your pet, everything was pre scripted *and there was nothing that should, could or would have been changed for the learning opportunities each of your souls chose to experience.*

Please Read that all again!!!

IF you still feel guilt, then examine what you learned from the experience. Your knowledge is the EXACT education you were supposed to learn from the lessons surrounding your pet's transition.

Take your newfound comprehension and realize your soul and life has evolved to a higher level. **Understanding "why"** a death occurred **is the Gift** contained within that traumatic event!!

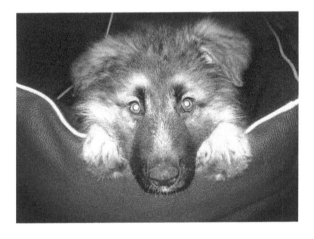

Reconnection

Prayer to find your pet:
I ask the energy formerly known as _____
to lead me to your new being in perfect timing. So be it, it is done. Thank you.

How do I find my pet?
Listen to and trust when and where your inner guidance leads. Do not delay the timing and guidance of your inner urgings when your heart compels or incessantly nags you to search for your new pet.
Act immediately!

You will instinctively "know" whether to look for a puppy, a rescue animal, in an animal shelter, on an internet search or in a newspaper ad. Follow your heart.

Your pet may just wander up and appear out of "nowhere." Someone may call you to "come see" this wonderful fur, finned or feathered creature that they saw, have found, are fostering or was "just turned in."
GO! Haven't you left yet?

Brent Atwater's
Just Plain Love® Books presents

If you are new to listening to your inner guidance, let's say this again:
Never overlook the little details and just pass them off as not worthy of attention.

Follow through on all information presented to you, **at the time it is presented** and trust it is correct. All those signs lead to your pet!
There are no coincidences!

Do NOT be discouraged by hearing "he's already taken or been adopted," or sold or not available.

If you KNOW in your heart that this is YOUR pet, be steadfast, keep going forward and do not be deterred by what you perceive as current roadblocks. Kim and Sidey's adventure are a great example of this principle.

If you don't have
that "**certain** knowing" in your heart
and or
the details don't work out for you to get a particular animal, then
the Universe is letting you know,
it's **NOT** your reincarnated pet!

If the Universe casts doubt in your heart, **then there is a reason.** Ask God/ the Universe to show you the information for your highest and best good. And no matter what, TRUST!!

When your pet has made all these efforts to return to you, **all things will just "work out" in some of the most interesting, amazing and _unbelievable_ ways so you can be together again!**

An "adopted" pet may never get picked up, a deposit never honored, people change their minds! The Universe will see that you are reunited one way or another! **You CAN'T mess it up!**

Recognition
THE number one question: **"Could I miss my pet?"**
NO! Nope, no way, no can do, huh uh, NOT!
Absolutely not! and NO!

Brent Atwater's
Just Plain Love® Books presents

The Universe insures you won't get the wrong pet! When it's the correct reincarnate, the Universe will arrange to <u>make all things possible</u> to bring your companion home!

IF you make the wrong choice, the Universe will disrupt the process to insure that you make the correct choice with perfect coincidences.

Like pre-birth contractions, the waves of energy during your pet's reentry will feel like inner guidance "contractions." The inspiration to search for them will increase in frequency. These "nudgies" compel and propel you until you DO reunite! It's like your insides won't leave you alone UNTIL you do, go or see what the Universe directs you towards!

THIS IS IMPORTANT: The first mistake you could make is - **in your loneliest moments** don't get caught in other people's opinions or swayed by ACs or advisors.

Always confirm what someone "tells you" or "communicates to you" inside your heart.

<u>ONLY your soul</u> is interwoven with your pet's energy. You and she/he are "One."

<u>Only YOU</u> will TRULY recognize his/her presence as a new incarnate.

I could FEEL Friend in my heart! However, I was so caught up and overwhelmed by my emotions that I missed seeing the "B" on his hip. My close friends, who were an **integral part** of my previous dog's life, upon seeing the video, immediately recognized that it was MY Friend returning home! I only "felt" it.

They pointed out that the white "B" in Friend's fur looked like my signature. Obviously, God knew I needed extra "in your face" "confirmation" signs!

ONLY you and perhaps those very close to your pet's soul when he/she was alive, will feel and know that true soul energy recognition!

The second biggest error recognizing your pet -HOPE and "missing your baby" with willful expectations that "he IS returning" that often overrides the truth that your pet is NOT going to come back. Some people decide when, what litter he will be born into, what she will look like and then proclaim it to be so. No matter how you justify or cling to the wish that you have a reincarnated pet with all sorts of signs, "my Guides told me so," "my AC told me so" or other self-explained erroneous information, it's just not so.

According to the scientific law of Physics, every living thing has a very specific individual energy pattern that makes up its unique identity. Look at and examine each animal's energy identification pattern. If the deceased or living pet's ID and the new or future animal's ID don't match, then that pet is not reincarnated. Throughout all of time, incarnation after incarnation, your pet's unique energy ID stays the same! It's just that simple.

THE BIGGEST ERROR of all!!! "He feels so familiar and almost looks like my deceased pet, plus I've gotten signs while I was looking for him and I hope I'm not wrong."

Many people mistake an animal from their deceased pet's Soul group as their reincarnated pet. The new animal feels very familiar because it has a similar vibrational pattern as the original being. It's like recognizing 2 sisters or cousins in the same family grouping. You recognize the connection to the original pet's energy although it is not your beloved companion.

If you look at each animal's energy, the two individual energy patterns when overlaid on one another do not match. The original pet's energy is a square peg and the new pet's energy looks like a round hole. However, both are in the same puzzle/ family/ Soul group.

When you look at a living or deceased pet's identification pattern and follow their energy into a future timeframe, if your pet is going to reincarnate, what you see is the exact energy pattern of the original pet replicated into the new reincarnated pet's body! A picture is worth a thousand heartbeats ☺

Ask yourself, are you processing the information available to you truthfully or clinging onto or manufacturing misinformation to satisfy your grief and longings? Sometimes saying to yourself "I hope I'm not making a mistake" is actually the true answer to your own question.

Whether your pet Returns from Rainbow Bridge or not, either way they have never stopped loving you and have never left your side. Your pet's Love is NEVER ending, forever and ALWAYS!

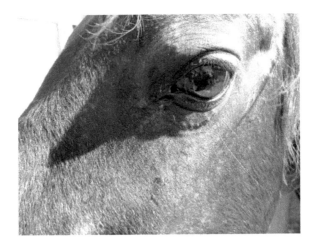

*I'm coming back to you
as soon as I can
from Rainbow Bridge!*

Confirmation: "How will I know him?"

Physical Characteristics
Eyes: It's **soul recognition**! Look into your pet's eyes, the windows of their soul. Your heart will **know** them and **feel** the connection you share and have shared.

Body:
Animals will always exhibit special (that only you will know) identifiable characteristics in the early weeks of arrival in your life to **ensure** you recognize them!

I prefer prick eared rough coated female red border collies. In his 5th reincarnation "B" Friend is a male (with lots of female tendencies) prick eared medium coated tri color. Close enough! ☺- Especially with that bright white "B" on his bottom identical to my signature! Hello! I recognized him!

Brent Atwater's
Just Plain Love® Books presents

One Saturday afternoon, a lady felt strong inner urges to drive to a shelter to find a dog to fill her heart's void until (she thought) her beloved pet reincarnated.

When she and her husband pulled into the parking lot, her soul recognition kicked in.

She saw a puppy that looked exactly like her old pet. He was walking across the parking lot toward the shelter on a leash with someone else!

"Coincidentally," the Universe had prearranged for this family to take her reincarnated puppy to the shelter at that precise moment to place the puppy for adoption.

Timing is everything! She immediately adopted HER dog!

Your pet may or may not have that same spot on their _____ in the same place like Carbon in *"I'm Home!"* Perhaps you will be given their physical description by an AC or AIH reading.

OR, your pet could be trying on a different look in this go round. Remember it's their choice.

ONLY embrace what resonates with you!

IF someone says your pet is coming back as a lop-eared squirrel and you don't think so. Ask your pet. Then go with YOUR instinct! After all, you're the parent! The Universe will provide every opportunity for you to know what they will look like!

Bonding and your Heart Connection

Your heart will recognize when you connect!

It's like a warm hug poured all over you. Your pet will start a bond with you right away, almost immediately. Even if they are a "walk-in "or "soul braid" you will still KNOW it's your pet as they make their spirit's transition while adjusting to their new body!

A client said it best "the moment I met Star, my heart stopped aching and my desire to stare at photos of my old dog lessened. I feel complete again.
Even though she is different on some levels, I still feel complete."

Your pet **will have** some different attributes in addition to the old ones! After all it's a new life to try new things!

Your pet will choose you.
They will choose you under any and all circumstances. They know you and there is no doubt about it when they pick you! This fact applies even if they are living with another individual before coming back into your life.

Judy visited her cousin and was adopted immediately by her cousin's Westie. After Judy left, that dog mourned, whined, would not eat, etc. Judy's cousin finally gave her the Westie for the "dog's sake." Loui was happily reunited with "her person" Judy for 17 more years.

Personality, behaviors and traits
Your new pet's quirky loveable habits and physical mannerisms will be uncannily similar, right down to:

Sleeping in the same location in "that funny position,"
Turning their head or walking with their tail held a certain way,
Liking or disliking the exact food (like eating ice cubes), or having an ear, rear end or tummy rubbed
Being Peculiar about their feet being touched, or whatever _____

Old Traits and New Attitudes

"New" animals **will act like an adult much sooner** than expected and display fewer "new baby" behaviors and attitudes.

A "walk in" or "over-soul" pet's mannerisms will be the same or VERY similar from the beginning. You'll have very few doubts that's it's your returned forever buddy!

When your pet comes back, they may take on a few new traits that you'd been hoping they would have. Pets will choose old and new qualities that are appropriate for and will contribute to your future path together. Plus they'll choose some different traits they want to try in a new life.

My previous "Sunday dogs" were never "child friendly" because they lived with a single adult.

New Friend is a people magnet. He thinks he's "human." The Universe obviously knew that this will be a wonderful trait for his paw/book signings, guest appearances for fundraising, pet therapy work and visitations in health care facilities!

Environment

Reincarnates respond immediately to all the old "things." They usually recognize all the old pet's toys, beds and other possessions.

They may even recognize their old home! Union Jack's story illustrates how a young pup recognized his old home. He tried to get out of the car while riding past his old home on the way to his person's new house!

Household Pets
Current household animals that lived with the deceased pet will recognize the "new" soul immediately. Reincarnates may even have similar grudges and disputes and dislikes or likes with the same pet.

Friend always got along with Mikey cat; however he never liked "Ugly, the most beautiful of them all." They still don't get along. I had hoped Heaven would have expanded his patience!

Reincarnated Pets remember Friends from a past life.

Do Pets respond to their old name or another phrase from their former life?
I've heard lots of stories about a new pet responding to an old pet's name. Some do, some don't!

While I was choosing a name for Friend, I'd use my sweetest come hither voice and read names to him for a response. NOT! He just kept walking away, playing with his toys and generally ignoring me.

So I said out loud, "maybe I should just call you

Friend like I my other dog!" He immediately got up and came over to me! Ask your pet what he/she would like to be called. You will hear the answer in your heart.

When your new pet responds to "love phrases" and "pet talk" that just you and your fur child knew, it's another way they let you know "I'm HOME!"

Reuniting!

No matter where your pet's energy is, whether they reincarnate or not, your beloved finned, furry or feathered soul companion will always be a part of your heart forever and always!!!

Love is never ending!
In your darkest hours after transition,
Choose Hope!
Your pet might be just a heartbeat away!

*Soon you'll feel **"I'm Home!"***
Pet Life after Death & Reincarnation is REAL!!! **Just ask** Friend,
the Dog with **my** "B" on His Bottom!

After Your Pet Returns!

Look at my face-
Of course
I'm Coming back from Rainbow Bridge!

In perfect timing, that moment arrives.

How long does it take to emotionally adapt?

"Although I know this is my pet reincarnated, sometimes it boggles my mind that his Soul is in this new body. I look at him and can't believe my eyes, but I know my heart feels whole again!"

Your pet will also question new surroundings as if they are trying to remember. It's interesting to watch as they stare at or sniff familiar past life territory or things in order to determine why it feels familiar. They are processing this new life as well as you.

"Sometimes I feel guilty and disloyal to my old pet by loving this new body. Is that normal?"
Perfectly normal! It takes about 6 months for your human mind and senses to comprehend and adapt to the wonderful concept of reincarnation.

Brent Atwater's
Just Plain Love® Books presents

Though your Soul completely understands this process there will be many times, even years later, when you just shake your head and feel this can't be. It's so wonderful and unbelievable and real.

Reincarnated Pet Traits are INTENSE!
1. You can see it in their eyes, there's a palpable intensity!
2. Their energy for and participating in life is WIDE OPEN, full throttle and never ending!
3. Everything is magnified in their behavior compared to your old pet.
4. They have some new habits and personality traits. You will never have an exact copy of your old pet: they need to live new experiences for their evolution. They come back to us not only for us, but also to grow as souls.
5. The one thing you can be certain is that "you will recognize him/her and you will feel that the bond between you two hasn't changed."

Enjoy!!!

Questions from the Audience

How can an animal be your Soul mate?
The dictionary defines a soul mate as "one of two beings compatible with each other in disposition, point of view, or sensitivity for whom you have a deep affinity." Some believe that a soul mate is a being with whom we have shared other lifetimes.
Below are 2 beautiful descriptions that say it all!:

Brent Atwater's
Just Plain Love® Books presents

A soul mate is:
1. "When we feel safe enough to open the locks, our truest selves step out and we can be completely and honestly who we are; we can be loved for who we are and not for who we're pretending to be. Each unveils the best part of the other. No matter what else goes wrong around us, with that one person we're safe in our own paradise. Our soul mate is someone who shares our deepest longings, our sense of direction. When we're two balloons, and together our direction is up, chances are we've found the right person. Our soul mate is the one who makes life come to life." -- Richard Bach
2. A being with "whom we feel profoundly connected, as though the communication and communing that take place between us were not the product of intentional efforts, but rather a divine grace. This kind of relationship is so important to the soul that many have said there is nothing more precious in life." -- Thomas Moore

Can we have more than one animal soul mate?
YES!!! A soul mate is a portion of all you are. That's why you can have several. However you can only have one Twin Flame which is your EXACT match and your soul's other half!

Someday my Twin Flame will return from Rainbow Bridge!

Animal Life after Death & Animal Reincarnation
Everything You Always Wanted to Know!

Can another Animal be my Pet's Twin Flame?
Yes! Just like Humans, animals can have twin flames too! Diane's Starlight and Buddy are perfect examples.

Do Pets Have Near Death Experiences?
Yes. Animal do have NDE's when they choose not to use that specific exit point to transition. Instead they just visit the other side and return.

Who makes the decision that the animal comes back?
Reincarnation is a free will soul contract between you and your pet. The Universe honors your choices.

Brent Atwater's
Just Plain Love® Books presents

Is the way pets die already picked?

Yes. Your pet chooses the most appropriate exit point timing to leave earth. Before this incarnation, you BOTH have chosen what will occur. That's why you understand and KNOW in your soul when "it's time."

If exit points are already pre-determined, why would our pets plan, in some or many cases, a painful and drawn-out death for themselves?

The death process is a LEARNING opportunity for you both! Perhaps it's about YOU learning to endure a life process. Always look for the learning opportunity is EVERYTHING in life!

When Mike died to activate my soul's purpose, I was crying. From the other side he said, "I did the hard part with the steering wheel in my chest, now you get a grip and use the gifts that my dying activated within you." And so I did.

Look for what YOU can contribute to helping others from the death that you experienced. Search for what YOU can contribute to benefit others from the knowledge that you gained surrounding that death. Focus on the good, NOT the horrific-- evolve beyond the circumstances. After all, LIFE is about change and evolving.

I feel guilt over the circumstances surrounding the death of my pet. Will my feelings affect its reincarnation?

No. All events and circumstances were exactly as they should be for highest good of all those involved. However, guilt and anger will affect and dilute your connection with him while he's on the other side

My heart tells me he still here. Would you tell him I love him and miss him so much and can't wait to see him again?

YOU can tell you pet that you love him and miss him. He has NEVER Left your side and Never stopped loving you.

He has just changed forms and can still hear EVERY word and thought you have! And participate in every activity without the burden of a physical body getting in his way!

YOU have to step over the speed bump of believing your pet is dead into understanding that your pet is NOW in a LIVING energy form! It's just the Fur suit that is gone.

Brent Atwater's
Just Plain Love® Books presents

What is the Number One Question you are asked in an Animal Communication Reading?
Clients want to know if "my pet is ok?" and I always say yes!!!!

You don't know me, are not in the same location, haven't met my pet or seen and touched his belongings. How can you read him?
Every living being has a unique vibrational frequency blueprint, like each station on a radio tuner.

Locating an animal or ANY energy form is comparable to tuning into a specific radio station within the Universe. However the reader must have the ability to receive and translate the precise animal energy bandwidth they are searching for, in order to read, interpret and supply correct information to you.

Most Communicators use their psychic ability to get impressions and feelings about your animal and then translate that into information. The strength of their signal determines their accuracy.

When I tune into a pet's or human's life force energy, I derive my information from **what I see**. Therefore personal belongings or location is not necessary.

Do you still conduct Animal Communication readings?
Yes, I love meeting pets and people. It's an honor to talk with dead pets so I can comfort and help heal their parent's heart. PLUS I learn something new every Reading!

How is your work different from a traditional Animal Communicator's work?
Unlike ACs who telepathically "talk" to pets through mental impressions, I look at and have a conversation with the actual dead pet's Spirit form or the live pet's Soul energy. I interview and talk with them face to face and not thru telepathic impressions.

Brent Atwater's
Just Plain Love® Books presents

What do you do in a reading? (We have a YT Video and Pet Life Radio show on this subject.)

1. I ask the pet to provide 3 signs that the client will recognize so we positively know we are connected to the correct pet.
2. I look at the pet's Spirit and have a conversation about that they want their pet parents to know and what is important to them in their current or pre death life.
3. I ask if they have had past lives with their person. I am visually shown a video of each of those lives which I describe to the client.
4. Then we discuss the transition.   I look inside the pet's body at the organs and determine how they died, if they were in pain and any other information the client wants to discuss surrounding the death.
5. During and after the pet's Spirit form (or energy) crosses the death line, I ask if they are going to come back/ reincarnate, in what timeframe, what age they will be, when they will arrive and where-- plus how the pet parent will find them.
6. If returning, I watch the pet's Spirit as it reformulates into the future physical being and describe their new body and characteristics so the client can identify their newly reincarnated pet.
7. If not reincarnating, I ask the deceased pet WHY? I explain that "why" so the client is comforted and understands the reason for sharing life together and the purpose and soul evolution learning opportunities of not having their pet back in their life.

Do you teach classes?
Yes, **Animal Reincarnation Communication**

ARC™ certified
Animal Life after Death & Reincarnation Communicator

I also teach **Animal Intuitive Healthcare & Healing -AIH** (How to see inside an animal's body to diagnose, treat and heal health issues)

> **Animal Intuitive Healthcare & Healing**
> AIH
> Animal Communication, Intuitive Diagnosis & Healing for Veterinarians, Assistants and Technicians
>
> How to See Inside an Animal's Body
> to Diagnose, Treat & Heal Health Issues
>
> Brent Atwater

Brent Atwater's
Just Plain Love® Books presents

Why are some animal communicators unable to determine if my pet is going to return?

A person who reads "energy" whether it's a psychic, medium, clairvoyant, intuitive or animal/ interspecies communicator can only "tune into" or telepathically connect with a person's or animal's vibrational frequency that they are **capable** of "receiving." Each communicator or intuitive *has a specific vibrational bandwidth range from which they are able to receive and gather information.* If your reader is unable to tune in to 100 AM i.e. Fido's station, then they do not get the same information as another communicator who CAN tune into your pet's frequency.

No reading is less or more important than another. It's the same with humans. Some readers are great, because they "get" your full station and give you a wonderful reading. Others can't provide a detailed reading because they can't completely tune into your station's frequency -like only picking up only a little bit of a radio station.

Why do different animal communicators give me conflicting information and details?

As stated earlier, each reader can ONLY get information from the energy channels they ARE ABLE to access. Readings vary because you get information from psychics who are connecting to different levels and amounts of your pet's energy. Each energy level connection provides ONLY a specific amount of information. The more levels a reader can connect with, the more details and accurate information you get!

What is the difference between human energy and animal energy?
Every living thing humans, animals, rocks, trees, water all have a specific energy pattern or an electromagnetic vibrational frequency range.

A healthy human frequency has an energy range of 68- 72 MHz FYI; each organ in your body had a specific vibrational identity. Vibrational medicine addresses correcting and reconfiguring unhealthy energy patterns to resolve health problems. There is more information online if you are interested.

Animal energy frequencies vibrate at a lower MHz level than human energy. That does not make them a lesser being. They simply have a lower frequency energy pattern.

What does the energy of a "walk in" animal look like?
As you watch an animal's life force energy cross over the death line and reassemble into sparkler form, a "walk in's" energy/Spirit does an immediate U turn and goes back over the death line into a current life and not into future energy. Why, because the host body is back in the pre death environment of the original pet. It's very interesting to watch! Then the Reader can describe the body that their Soul has inhabited so you will know "where your pet went." ☺

What happens to animals left in shelters, do they reincarnate?
Location does not determine or effect any spiritual arrangement. Any animal anywhere can create a soul's contract to reincarnate if it's a mutual choice with an individual or a singular incarnation that is part of the animal's soul path.

Brent Atwater's
Just Plain Love® Books presents

Do service and guide dogs reincarnate?
Reincarnation is each individual animal's choice.

Do pets on the other side educate and direct animals on earth?
Yes. That is called an "over soul" agreement. The deceased pet directs and guides the living animal on "what to do" and "how to behave" from Heaven.

Some animals on the other side assist pets during the death and transition process including after they have crossed the Rainbow Bridge.

Do pet's spirits visit earth and interact with animals they have previously known?
Yes. Animals live by their keen instincts. They are very aware of energies and entities from across the veils. Often times your earth pet will continue to "play" or interact with the deceased animal's living energy. They may growl over the food bowl at an imaginary friend, or bat a paw at a plain air playmate.

Do animals come back and remember their past life?
In my opinion they do remember past lives, that's why they recognize you!

When live pets play with deceased animals' energy, is that a sign that the pet in spirit is going to reincarnate?
No. It's just a sign that animals are very aware of "all there is."

Could the physical hardship my pet experienced before death, stop their reincarnation in this lifetime?
All death events are exit point choices made by the pets and humans involved. Each death scenario is a

Brent Atwater's
Just Plain Love® Books presents

learning opportunity for their souls.
If the pet chooses to wait until a later reincarnation, that's the exception. Either way, the spiritual agreement between the two of you must be fulfilled at some point in eternity.

I lost my job and my pet. Does she understand my situation? Can I ask her not to reincarnate?
Because you and your pet are heart connected she understands YOU and your needs. If it's in your highest and best good or a learning opportunity, the Universe will offer you choices of what is best for **both** of you. Your pet's return and agreement is based upon sharing life's journey **together**. You can request a change of incarnations, but it's HER choice.

Why do you use the word Transition?
First, the word transition is softer and gentler than "put down", death or euthanized, and it is factually correct. During the death process a pet's energy does transition from Earth to Heaven or "all there is" in the Universe.

When the physical body (finned, feathered or fur suit) ceases to exist the Pet's Soul energy which inhabited the Earth form then changes over into another energy form/ being on the other side of the veil.

By thinking of death as a transition, you become more aware of the reality that energy never dies it just changes form! Embracing the transition perspective may also allow the physical death to be a little less painful or traumatic when you understand death is not really a forever ending.

I share custody of a pet. Will it reincarnate back to me? The pet will reincarnate back to the individual with whom it shares a spiritual contract.

Will my pet reincarnate to another person?
NO. Any pet's reincarnation contract is a one on one soul agreement with a specific person- you. Pets do not reincarnate to another person.

IF a pet decides to return to the earth school for a singular soul's evolution, it does not affect any contracts filled or unfilled that the two of you have together. He'll just hang out on earth to learn his lessons and won't have that "heart connection" with anyone. It's like going to class, but not being in love with the teacher.

Most people have experienced a wonderful pet, but the soul connection was not there. That's when the animal is on their own learning path and isn't in a lifetime with a reincarnation contract.

Brent Atwater's
Just Plain Love® Books presents

Does anything ever go wrong when a pet is reincarnating?
Only the free will choice of you and your pet can affect the reincarnation process.

Often a grieving pet owner will ask the pet to return before Universal "perfect timing." If the pet chooses to honor the pet parent's request, most times the consequences are less than desirable due to health issues or life span on earth.

Since there are no coincidences, the pet parent usually learns from this rushed incarnation, to Trust that all Universal timing is perfect. Sadly they also may not be with their pet again in that lifetime!

Asking a pet to "do something" not in your original plan, can slow down their energy.

Trust!

When your Pet Returns from Rainbow Bridge They WILL find YOU!

Do abused animal come back?
Abuse is not a factor in a reincarnation contract.

If I clone a pet, will it have the soul of my original pet?
Cloning does NOT guarantee the new body will have the original pet's soul. If your pet contracted to return, it may or may not choose to use the clone as its new vehicle.

Can you tell it's my reincarnated pet's energy if they are still in the womb?
Yes! I see their energy inside the Mother's body.

When does a pet's energy enter into the new body?
That is determined by the Soul agreement you have with the pet. If it's a walk in, the transfer is immediate. In a soul braid the transfer and rewiring takes time over several weeks. A new body's energy comes in when the fetus is forming.

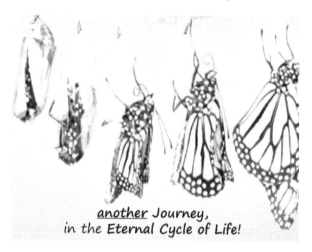
another Journey, in the Eternal Cycle of Life!

I neutered my dog. He ran away and won't come home. Does this affect his reincarnating to me? No! A spiritual contract is based on a soul to soul agreement, not a medical procedure.

My pet was lost. Does that affect reincarnation?
Even if you "lost" your pet, that script was "preplanned." The manner in which your pet chose to exit your life will not affect any previous agreements.

Brent Atwater's
Just Plain Love® Books presents

If I know my pet is reincarnating, should I give up the grief process all together?
No. The stages of grief are a normal and beneficial response to loss and part of the human emotional evolvement journey.

Can a pet's soul energy inhabit multiple animals and simultaneously reincarnate into different bodies at the same time?
No. In my research I do NOT find this to be true with the laws of physics and energy. To be alive and well, a physical body HAS to have and maintain a certain vibrational frequency (MHz) to will support a healthy biological being.

IF you divide a total life force/ soul energy into multiple parts, each segment's frequency would be lowered by that division. The original "whole soul" maintained a specific healthy vibrational to stay alive. Therefore every particle of the fractional whole would not be able to to sustain life in an earth body due to its lower vibration.

It's a great concept in "psychic" thought, but looking at the physics of real energy- it's a deadly proposition!

Parallel lives is a good mental concept, but not in actually living on earth and sustaining existence. That's why individuals who try to leave their bodies or teleport often get very sick! Physical energy is physical energy that can NOT be altered beyond certain frequency levels or death occurs.

That's also the reason that at some biological point a person can NOT regenerate from a disease. When the physical vibrational energy lowers to a certain level within a soul's housing-- that soul - spirit leaves which means biological death.

Some people have mind traveled for so long outside of their body (unknowing about leaving it without a living frequency) that when they returned, their body's vital functions had shut down and their body is dead! Whoops!

Souls can be all over the place in "all there is" but not when it's housed on earth in a body!

If I freeze my pet's body for the taxidermist, will it affect her reincarnation? No! You need to take her body to the taxidermist immediately so bacteria will not destroy her tissue or infect your freezer.

What's the difference between Pet Afterlife and Animal Life after Death?
Afterlife is the description of an environment we've designated for a pet's spirit who stays and lives "on the other side" or "in the afterlife" or "at Rainbow

Bridge" or "in all there is." Animal Life after Death is the timeframe when an animal leaves their "afterlife residence" and joins the 30 to 40% of pet Souls that reincarnate or come back to Earth for another life (after their previous death) to have more learning opportunities for their Souls' evolution.

And last but not least

Can you tell if a LIVING animal is reincarnated or will reincarnate?
Yes. See our YouTube video of a "Live Pet's Reincarnation Reading!" and others. I just look at and follow a living pet's past energy to determine when or if they have been with you before. OR I look into the future to see if they are going to reincarnate to be with you again!

All sadness is gone...

Your heart is whole again!!

True pet Reincarnation Stories in our companion books!

* More Resources Pet life after death *

1. Facebook Pet Loss Group -Ask questions in the World's # 1 Pet Loss, Animal life after death and Reincarnation Group.

2. Pet Loss Radio: "Alive Again" on www.PetLifeRadio.com show

3. Pet Loss TV
   YouTube Channel -Brent Atwater

4. Blog: http://petreincarnation.blogspot.com
Share your stories

5. Workshops, Events / Live Q & A Chats
are announced on Brent Atwater Pet Loss Page.
https://www.facebook.com/#!/Petsloss

6. Events: Want an Event in your area,
email us!

7. Newsletter

8. Memorial Rainbow Wristband:
Engraved:
My Love is Never Ending. I'm coming back to YOU!™ which can be found on our websites.

9. Readings for Rescue™ Ms. Atwater uses her Gifts to raise funds for Rescue and Animal welfare organizations. Email us to create an Event for you.

VIDEOS: Return from Rainbow Bridge
in 10+ languages at
http://www.youtube.com/user/BrentAtwater

POEMS: Return from Rainbow Bridge
Download and print out in YOUR language at
www.justplainlovebooks.com

Return from Rainbow Bridge Facebook page
Please Like us and share with your friends. Pass the love and awareness forward!

Message to Book Clubs, Retail Stores, Professional Associations & Organizations

Ms. Atwater will be delighted to speak with your group over the phone or schedule a presentation or event.

Email us at
Brent@BrentAtwater.com
BrentAtwater@live.com

Brent Atwater

Authority on Animal life after death & Reincarnation
Pioneer & Founder-Animal Intuitive Healthcare & Healing

Brent Atwater (and "Friend" her dog with a "B" on his Bottom) is the world's authority on pet loss, animal life after death and reincarnation. Brent's readings are filled with very personal information and specific details that capitvate clients and audiences worldwide.

Ms. Atwater has the extraordinary gift to see inside a body to accurately diagnose current and future health issues and to create healing solutions.

At age 5 Brent's intuitive talents were discovered by Duke University's Dr. J B Rhine the founder of ESP in his initial investigations. Ms. Atwater's specialized intuitive diagnostic abilities have earned her the

Brent Atwater's
Just Plain Love® Books presents

nickname of the "human MRI."

Her world renowned Medical Intuitive practice has highly respected, evidence based, documented and published case studies. Brent can see the organs, nerves, bones, tissue et al inside your body, plus diagnose and predict future events. Therefore Ms. Atwater can determine if and when your pet is going to reincarnate and what they will look like!

Brent's healing work regenerating her dog's spinal cord nerves and vertebra has been documented by NC State University's School of Veterinary Medicine. She has been a speaker and teacher for the NC Veterinary Association and taught at the New York Open Center. For decades Ms. Atwater has pioneered and founded AIH the field of Animal Intuitive Healthcare & Healing. Her Medical Intuitive Diagnosis MIDI and AIH books are groundbreaking resource books for the science of Medical Intuition and Healing Animals with Integrative Energy Medicine.

In 1987 Brent founded the *Just Plain Love*® Charitable Trust. After law school and the death of her fiancé, Brent refocused her career on helping pets and their people heal. Ms. Atwater has authored 10 *Just Plain Love*® Books with more to follow.

Ms. Atwater has devoted decades to researching pet life after death, pet reincarnation and human animal spiritual contracts which produced multiple books whose titles are translated into other languages.

Brent is a true animal lover who offers us the benefit of her incredible gifts and her passion to help heal and uplift the lives of pets and their people! Her mission is to ignite hope and healing in people after pet loss in addition to activating and empowering every person's inherent abilities and Gifts.

Ms. Atwater is also a pioneer in healing art medicine by scientifically documenting the healing energy, diagnostic abilities and healing benefits of her *Paintings That Heal®* (www.BrentAtwater.com). She is one of the contemporary American painters who are bringing forth a new cultural renaissance by blending her classical artistic training with spirituality and energy infused into her healing art.

Brent Atwater's life work facilitates positive and transformative results!

"Friend" is the co-host of the Pet life after death & Reincarnation shows. He is a Red tri colored Border collie. Friend "B"elieves his mission is to expand awareness about animal reincarnation to help heal hearts. When he's not assisting Brent with paw signings, pet fund raising events or practicing hugs and kisses for his pet therapy work, Friend enjoys being spoiled, herding fish and turtles in his pond and playing with his "Mister Bears."

Brent Atwater's
Just Plain Love® Books presents

The Just Plain Love® *Story*

"Experiencing a pediatric intensive care, oncology, burn or trauma unit to me, is a soul wrenching jolt to anyone's world. I had to summon all my "heart" to handle the various states of disrupted life. Right then and there I decided that a positive Light needed to shine on the hearts and minds of these struggling little souls, so new to earth and so old to the diseases, health issues and medical conditions whose very procedures and treatments ravaged their young bodies.

I decided that I was going to find a way to offer a "positive spin" on all of the health issue negatives and to create a portal of communication and a treasure of heartwarming and reassuring perspectives to those "hands off" subjects.

Additionally I want to inspire a muffled laugh, instigate a tiny smile, mischievous giggle or just create an environmental change and safe place for even a brief moment that would add a sparkle to a weary eye.

AND I was going to give a comforting and supportive symbolic "hug" to each patient and reader by filling them with a sense of pride in themselves for having endured their own health battle and surrounding issues. Plus, I would provide a tangible and permanent way to honor and celebrate their courage!

I was unable to have children, so this is my way of giving back.
In 1987 the Just Plain Love® Charitable Trust was born."

Brent Atwater's Other Dream:
Just Plain Love® Plays, Performances & Educational Programs for Children with "Poof" the Angel & "Friend" the pet angel therapy dog.

Surely, Ms. Atwater dreams, there can be participatory mini skits/plays held in healthcare and medical facilities lasting about 5 to 15 minutes that would hold a patient's attention, entertain, educate, rehabilitate and provide a few safe moments of mental relief through laughter, plus providing each patient with a tangible Badge of Honor to reward and recognize their courage.

For the past 20+ years Brent Atwater has researched, tested, rewritten and reworked each children's healing book and play according to the storytelling responses and reactions from healthy and unhealthy readers, caregivers, family, friends, medical and healthcare professionals, clients and her storytelling audience.

Brent Atwater's hope is to inspire the creative imagination of readers of all ages to replace negative thoughts about health issues, medical experiences, rehabilitative therapy and reentry into society with a positive "spin" on their journey to health and well-being.

Visit
www.BrentAtwater.com

Join Brent Atwater's & Friend's Global Community on Twitter, Facebook, YouTube, Instagram, Pinterest, MySpace and others

Just Plain Love® Books

inspiring thoughts that provide smiles, hugs and
healing for every reader's heart!

Other Just Plain Love® Titles

Inspirational:
The Beach Book: Beach Lessons for a Workaholic!

Children's Books:
Cancer Kids—God's Special Children!
Cancer and MY Daddy

Life and Spiritual Purpose:
How to Accept, Trust & Live Your Life's Spiritual
        Purpose: Am I Worthy?
Prayers to Empower Your Life's Spiritual Purpose

Energy Medicine, Intuitive Development:
Medical Intuition, Intuitive Diagnosis, MIDI- How to
        See Inside a Body to Diagnose, Treat & Heal
AIH - Animal Intuitive Healthcare & Healing
          for Veterinarians, Assistants & Technicians

Self Help and Healing, Mind Body Medicine:
Healing Yourself! 23 Ways to Heal YOU!
Paintings that Heal! Art is the Medicine

**Pet Loss, Afterlife, Pet Life after Death and
Animal Reincarnation:**
the Dog with a "B" on His Bottom!
"I'm Home!" a Dog's Never Ending Love Story
"I'm Home!" a Cat's Never Ending Love Story
"I'm Home!" a Horse's Never Ending Love Story
Pet Loss, Afterlife & Pet life after death
        Answers for all your heart's Questions!
La Réincarnation des Animaux de Compagnie
動物は生まれ変わる

We hope you enjoyed
our
Just Plain Love® Book.

Visit Brent Atwater's website:
http://www.BrentAtwater.com

Connect with Brent Atwater's Global Community
in our Facebook Groups & Pages and on Instagram, Pinterest, Twitter, YouTube, LinkedIn MySpace and more...

This material is internationally copyrighted with all rights reserved to B. Brent Atwater. None of this material may be used or reproduced without written permission of B. Brent Atwater. Animal Life after Death & Animal Reincarnation Everything you always wanted to know! © 2008-2015 R1

Lightning Source UK Ltd.
Milton Keynes UK
UKHW021830060320
359912UK00017B/206